MW00412115

Live!
Love!
Laugh!
Laughlin!

"The Dream Continues in Paradise!"

by Father Charlie Urnick

Copyright © 2013 Father Charlie Urnick

All rights reserved.

ISBN: 1480214604

ISBN 13: 9781480214606

This is a collection of sermons given at St. John the Baptist Catholic Church in Laughlin, Nevada from July 2009 until July 2010. To hear the current sermons, please join us for Mass. We love company! Our Weekend Mass schedule is as follows:

Saturday 4:00 PM
Mass at Don's Celebrity Theatre in the Riverside Resort, Laughlin, Nevada

Saturday 6:00 PM
Mass at St. John the Baptist Catholic Church, 3055 El Mirage Way, Laughlin, Nevada

Sunday   8:00 AM
Mass at St. John the Baptist Catholic Church 3055 El Mirage Way, Laughlin, Nevada

Sunday   10:00 AM
Mass at Don's Celebrity Theatre in the Riverside Resort, Laughlin, Nevada

Sunday   12:00 Noon
Mass at Don's Celebrity Theatre in the Riverside Resort, Laughlin, Nevada

St. John the Baptist Catholic Church
P.O. Box 31230
Laughlin Nevada 89028

Copyright 2013 - No portion of this book may be reprinted or copied by any means, mechanical or electronic, without the express written permission of the author.

✠✠✠

Diocese of Las Vegas
P.O. BOX 18316
LAS VEGAS, NEVADA 89114-8316

OFFICE OF
THE BISHOP
(702) 735-9608
FAX (702) 735-8941

January 3, 2013

Reverend Charles Urnick
Administrator
St. John the Baptist
P. O. Box 31230
Laughlin, NV 89028

Dear Father Urnick:

After consultation with Right Reverend Archimandrite Francis Vivona, Censor Librorum for the Diocese of Las Vegas, I give you ecclesiastical approval for the book *"Live! Love! Laugh! Laughlin"* for public use among the faithful.

I do think it would be valuable to add in the very beginning of your manuscript that you are a retired priest of the Archdiocese of Newark who is serving the parishioners of St. John the Baptist in Laughlin as it would give the reader a better tone of who you are and what you are doing in Laughlin.

Nihil Obstat:	Right Reverend Archimandrite Francis Vivona, STM, JCL
Imprimatur:	Most Reverend Joseph A. Pepe, D.D., J.C.D.
Date:	January 3, 2013

Wishing you the best, I remain

Sincerely yours in Christ,

+

Most Reverend Joseph A. Pepe, D.D., J.C.D.
Bishop of Las Vegas

JAP/pb

C: Right Reverend Archimandrite Francis M. Vivona, S.T.M., J.C.L.

The **"Nihil Obstat"** and **"Imprimatur"** are official declarations that a book or pamphlet is free of doctrinal or moral error. No implication is contained therein that those who have granted the "Nihil Obstat" and the "Imprimatur" agree with the content, opinions or statements expressed.

To All Who Read This Book -

I am the happiest Catholic priest in the whole world! I was ordained as a Catholic priest in New Jersey on May 25, 1974 and I have completed 38 years as a priest. My current assignment is **Paradise**, otherwise known as Laughlin, Nevada! I have been assigned here as Administrator of St. John the Baptist Catholic Church since July 1, 2008. As far back as I can remember, my dream has been to serve as a priest in the Diocese of Las Vegas, and here I am living my dream along the banks of the beautiful Colorado River! Yes, this is really **Paradise** for me!

Many years ago, a Las Vegas performer (David Kesterson) shared a thought with me, and I have used that thought as my attitude towards living my life. My assignment in Laughlin fits that thought so perfectly that my brother/friend Thom suggested that I incorporate that thought into my title for this book. So please enjoy reading this book: **LIVE! LOVE! LAUGH! LAUGHLIN! "The Dream Continues in Paradise!"** Believe me, I have enjoyed writing this book almost as much as I have enjoyed living it!

Welcome to my world!

I have always been blessed with happiness because of the amazing people in my life, and since this book is the second one I have ever written **(and hopefully not the last!)**, I really want and need to single out some of those amazing people for praise and thanks:

- My Mom and Dad who brought me into this world a long time ago. My Dad lived to see me almost complete my teenage years. He died in 1967 when I was 19 years old. My Mom lived to see me ordained as a priest and shared so much of my love for Las Vegas, Laughlin and all of Nevada throughout the years. My Mom died in 2006, but she is very much a part of my life even now. There is a very special bond between a mother and her son. **Ask any son, or any mother, and they know.**

- The parishioners of St. John the Baptist Catholic Parish in Laughlin, Nevada, who give me so much hope and joy and love, and who have to listen to me preach almost every weekend of the year! I first called Laughlin **"Paradise"** in my sermon on 23 November 2008! And it will be **"Paradise"** forever in my mind until I get to the OTHER Paradise (Heaven)!

- The snowbirds and visitors who come to Laughlin from all over the world and who worship with us either at our church on the hill or in the Riverside casino, and who bring me bulletins and news from churches around the world.

- My brother **Michael** who really has been one of the best and most influential behind-the-scenes forces in my life, always encouraging me to be my best self, patiently (sometimes) calling me to account when I am not, and always inspiring me to see and hear elements of life I might never have noticed without him. It is undeniably true that it is to Michael that I owe the push to actually sit down and write my first book. And I equally owe Michael the credit for encouraging/prodding/pushing/shoving me to write this book! Michael is really and truly the best brother a guy could ever have! **Michael, I'm so blessed and so glad we're family!** You sometimes have the wisdom of Solomon to share with me in my life! And **sometimes**, I really do listen to you!

- My "illegitimate son" **Eddie** who shows up on several pages of this book because his genuine goodness and youthful enthusiasm make me the proudest Pa in the world. **Eddie is clearly my much-loved "illegitimate son!"** Because of him, I have learned so much about the incredible joys and worries of being a father with a small **"f"** which in turn, I think, has made me a better Father with a capital **"F"** for my parishioners! There's an old saying that if you love someone, you sometimes want to kill him. I love you, son! (NLPLC). **Eddie, I'm so blessed and so glad we're family!**

- My weird nephew/other son **Andy** who discovered his Las Vegas family on his way to LA a few years ago. Eddie and Andy had been roommates and friends and brothers for almost forever, so it was very natural that Andy should move into our family. **Andy, I'm so blessed and so glad we're family!**

- The four of us - **Myself, Michael, Eddie and Andy** - have chosen to be more than friends. **We've chosen to be family.** If you can appreciate what that means to me, no further explanation is necessary. If you can't appreciate what that means to me, no further explanation is possible.

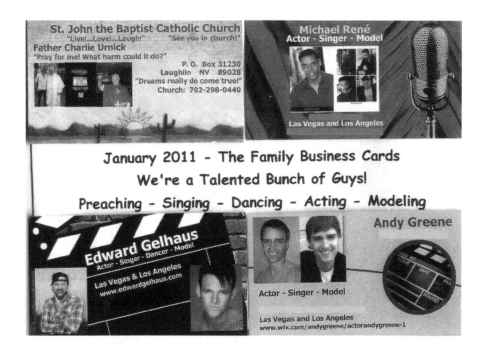

- My friends **Paul** and **Charlie** who keep me honest and truthful and smiling and hugged. I don't think they realize how much their friendship has contributed to my life, but I owe them big time, **really big**

time! They are really the very first friends I made in Las Vegas when I moved out West in 2008.

- My friend, **Bruce Ewing**, whose own writings online are so good and so inspirational for me to read, and who shares a beautiful outlook on life and grace with me. From **"Forever Plaid"** to the days of the **"Phat Pack"**, Bruce continues to be an influence for good in my life!

- My friend **Mike**, from the **Mike Hammer Comedy Magic Show** up in Las Vegas is an truly outstanding example of God putting the best people into my life. Talented, funny, sincere, giving, and so many other adjectives describe him so well. I can't begin to add up how many Tuesday or Wednesday nights I have spent laughing and smiling and eating and just hanging out with him and **Andrew** on Fremont Street this past year!

- And here in Laughlin, I have to single out **Thom** and **Jason,** who have become so much more than friends and walking partners. These two guys have gotten me to do things that I've never dreamed of doing! Things like sit-ups, jogging, eating sushi, and so much more! I figure God wanted me to have two local brothers, so He gave me these two guys to keep me level-headed and humble, and not ever let me become proud! I must have done something right in life to deserve them being in my life now.....or maybe I'm in their lives as payback for something terrible they did in their past! **Either way, I'm glad we're in Laughlin together now.**

- And also in Laughlin, **Steve**, who gets dragged into so many of my local parish adventures, yet never complains and always helps to make the adventures a lot of fun. I think I've eaten meals with Steve more than anyone else out here!

- The priests of my past who taught me so much by their preaching, and so much more by their lives: Father Charlie O'Connor, Msgr. Tom Kleissler, Father Ed Duffy, Father Gerry McGarry, Msgr. Dave Casazza, Father Francis Byrne, Father Ken St. Amand, Msgr. James Turro, Father Chuck McCusker, Father Charlie Hudson, Msgr. Peter O'Connor, Msgr. Caesar Orrico, Msgr. Mike Fitzpatrick, Msgr. Charles Lillis, Father Robert Hunt, Father Ed Ciuba, Msgr. Harold Darcy, Father Steve Feehan, Msgr. Carl Hinrichsen, and Father Edward Hinds.

- And all those people who have ever said to me on their way out of Mass here in Laughlin: **"Have you ever thought of putting your sermons together in a book?"** Well, for a second time now, I have!

I began serious work on this collection of sermons from my second year in Laughlin back in January 2012, and I completed the basic structure by the summer of 2012, spending almost six months revising and revisiting a year of sermons at St. John the Baptist Catholic Church in Laughlin. It has definitely been a labor of love doing this! For those who hear me regularly, you will recognize the development of some common themes and messages. You will see some wonderfully awesome recurring characters in my sermons because they are in my life.

I never have to make up my stories, they happen to me!

Welcome to my world!

Most of my sermon material is purely original, but sometimes it has been inspired by things I have seen or read in books, magazines, newspapers and on the internet. I apologize if I have inadvertently used someone else's material without giving proper credit. I do occasionally read sermon ideas by Father Anthony Kadavil online and the works of Father Anthony de Mello always provide inspiration in this book.

A portion of the profits from the sale of this book **($1.00 from every book sold)** will be donated to St. John the Baptist Catholic Church to assist in the current works and activities of the best little parish in the world! We are proud to be a little outpost of the Diocese of Las Vegas serving all those who live in or visit Laughlin, and the surrounding communities in Nevada, Arizona, and California.

Over the years, I've collected a number of sayings which I have found to be helpful, humorous, thoughtful and guiding. I gladly share them with you at the start of this journey through my second year in Laughlin and the entire year that follows. Perhaps reading some of these sayings might prepare you for the mind and spirit behind the sermons that follow. I hope you enjoy the journey with me, it's going to be an awesome ride! If you liked my first book **DREAMS REALLY DO COME TRUE!**, then I think it is a safe bet that you will like this new book **LIVE! LOVE! LAUGH! LAUGHLIN!** just as much! Some of these sayings appeared in my first book, but I love them so much that I want to repeat them here!

"I wouldn't like to have lived without ever having disturbed anyone!" (Catherine Doherty)

"Relationships are built on trust; trust begins by sharing." (Christian Mueller)

"Laughter is the sound of assumptions breaking." (Michael Goudeau)

"For personal growth, you should do something every day that scares you!" (Kevin Lynch...as he coaxed me onto his Harley!)

"Consider any man that you can help your friend, and double friend that man so selfless as to offer help to you." (Rod McKuen)

"I think when you are somewhere, you oughta be there, 'cause it's not about how long you stay in a place, it's about what you do while you're there. And when you go, will the place where you've been be any better off for your having been there?" (Chris Stevens/John Corbett in the show "Northern Exposure")

"Someday, we'll look back on this, laugh nervously, and change the subject!" (Ken Mason)

"Live!...Love!...Laugh!" (David Kesterson)

"There is nothing wrong with pointing out the flaws of people you care about as long as you are in their lives long enough to assist them in overcoming their flaws." (Michael Rene Serrano, 25 July 2009)

"Of course you did!"....."Really?" (Michael Rene Serrano)

"You're stuck with me - wherever I go, whatever I do - you're coming along for the ride!" (Eddie Gelhaus, 29 March 2010))

"Haha! I'll deny the stories and burn the pics!" (Andy Greene, 30 September 2010)

"If you're ever in a jam, I'll be there to lend a helping hand." (Jason Haskins, 6 August 2012)

"Let's put our heads together and really get him..... You appear to be a member of the Insane Clown Posse.....A new low, even for you." (Thom Armstrong, 18 August 2012)

"**THAT** may cause pain!" (Thom Armstrong, 23 November 2012) I need to note that the word **"THAT"** appears nearly **100** times **LESS** in this book than it did in the manuscript version which Thom proofread for me! Thanks for **THAT**, Thom!

"Pray for me! What harm could it do?" (Father Charlie)

"See you in church!" (Father Charlie)

"Be good, be strong, be you!" (Father Charlie)

"It's so nice...It must be Paradise!" (Father Charlie)

"Dreams really do come true!" (Father Charlie)

"Live!...Love!...Laugh!...Laughlin!" (Father Charlie)

This is a review of my first book.
You may find some insight into my style and my dreams here!

DREAMS REALLY DO COME TRUE! :
My First Year in Paradise (Laughlin, Nevada)
by Father Charlie Urnick (Published February 19, 2011)
Reviewed by Jim M. Guynup, Christ the King Parish,
Las Vegas, Nevada

In the southern tip of Nevada, there lies a town about 90 minutes from the center of Las Vegas where a man named Don Laughlin bought this piece of land by the Colorado River in 1964 and founded the Riverside Casino at which he then offered a complete chicken dinner for 98 cents! And despite his not wanting it, the townfolk insisted on calling it Laughlin. Over 50 years later a vivacious priest with an effervescent smile starts his love affair with Laughlin. He was ordained 1974 in New Jersey where he demonstrated his love for preaching and teaching for over 34 years. Then a lifelong dream became reality when his prayers were answered and he was transferred to Laughlin in the Diocese of Las Vegas.

Father Charlie Urnick loves to preach and write and one can easily feel that with every word he says or writes. His first venture in book-writing includes his sermons from 2008-2009 which have been described by Amazon.com as **"folksy wisdom"** and to that I would like to add if you enjoyed Fulton J. Sheen, then reading this book is an absolute must!

What Father Charlie manages to do is make relevant the readings in the liturgical year plus inject humor and add some love for his beloved Laughlin, including the food and then maybe even give us a household tip! For instance, one that I have since shared with many friends: **"If you cannot find your car in the parking lot, just put the keychain up to your chin and press the sounding button and with your body as the external antenna, it will find your car immediately"**

Father Charlie Urnick addresses all types of issues including trust, love, death, plants, Las Vegas, Lent, and, yes, even casinos, and the origin of Angel Food cake. He has many photos of his various adventures though I wish some of them could have been in color. Maybe next time hopefully. Since he also had a distinguished career in the Air Force, hopefully the next one that he is now planning will include more of that.

What struck me most about the book is his appreciation for many things that we take for granted, whether it is his love for a favorite food or the beauty of his town. His words about Laughlin and about our Catholic Christian Faith come so alive in this book that I hope each of you will experience it yourselves for a truly memorable summer reading experience.

14th Sunday in Ordinary Time - "B"

5 July 2009

FIRST READING: Ezekiel 2:2-5
PSALM: Psalm 123:1-4
SECOND READING: 2 Corinthians 12:7-10
GOSPEL: Mark 6:1-6

In the Gospel today, Jesus comes home to His own town of Nazareth, but He is not well-received by the townsfolk who feel they know where He is from and how limited His background is.

Another awesome week in Paradise! Temperatures hit 115 degrees one day this week, so we're finally warming up a bit! Enjoyed some homemade ravioli stuffed with spinach and cheese, some angel-food cake layered with sherbet, and an amazing grilled chicken citrus salad. Played some cards with some parishioners **(and lost!).** Got asked to bless a fish, and to bury a horse. And even turned down an invitation by David Copperfield to attend a movie. But it was at midnight and I really wanted to get some sleep. How many folks ever get to say that they turned down an invitation from David Copperfield?

And I got visited by a priest and some members of a religious group from out-of-state. They came for Mass and then we talked.....and they promised to pray for me. After I thanked them, they said they would be praying for me to have **courage** since I had to live here with **all this sin!** They had visited a casino in Laughlin and told me that they saw **"all those pathetic old people putting money into machines and they don't know God!"** My immediate response was **"Those pathetic old people are my parishioners!"** But then I gave a better defense! My experience here in Laughlin has been different. I don't feel that I'm surrounded by sin, and I certainly don't feel like I have to deal with **"pathetic old people"** who don't know God! So I just smiled and knew that as I begin my second year here there's one more priest who doesn't want to take my place, and eat my food, and have all this fun with my parishioners in Paradise! So if anyone ever tells you that it's boring to be a priest, have them come and talk with me. That was my week!

I love to travel and sometimes I get to meet some amazing people along the way. Back in 2006 while I was in New Jersey, I got an email which began: **"Do you believe in magic? Do you believe in miracles? You don't know who this is now, but you will at the end of this email."** Well, it sounded like one of those chain letters. But I read on: **"Do you remember being at the Gold River Casino in Laughlin, Nevada, in August, 1997?"** Now I'm thinking this might be an attempt at blackmail! But I read on: **"You came to see my magic show and wrote me a letter telling me how much you enjoyed it. I just got your letter this week - nine years later!"** The letter had fallen behind some furniture and was only discovered by an employee who happened to have worked there all these years. He was able to track down the magician to whom my letter had been addressed. He had moved back to Massachusetts to care for his Dad who had had a stroke and was in the beginning stages of alzheimer's. The magician whose stage name is **FLASH** had checked on the Internet and found that I was still at the same parish in New Jersey. A few weeks later, after a lot of emails and talking on the phone, we got to meet each other. We went out for dinner and stayed up until 4:30 AM the next morning talking about Las Vegas and Laughlin and magic and our lives. I like to think that God had this all planned out when our paths had crossed nine years earlier here in Laughlin, Nevada, so that we could meet up in 2006 on the East Coast. The opportunity to share with each other about his Dad and my Mom both having alzheimer's was really great for both of us. Flash was in town this week, and we had a great time up in Vegas for two days. This is just one of my **TRAVEL STORIES**.....and I've got thousands more!

I REALLY LOVE TO TRAVEL, and I suspect Jesus loved to travel too. So many of the Gospels are about His journeys throughout Judea, Samaria and Galilee. They tell us of the cures He worked, the people He visited, the teachings He gave in the various places throughout the ancient land of Israel. But today's Gospel is different. Jesus comes **HOME** to His own area, to His own hometown, to His own place of worship. If we were reading this Gospel passage for the first time, we might logically expect that here in Nazareth Jesus would work His greatest miracles. But exactly the opposite is true. Jesus did very little in the way of preaching or teaching or curing the sick in His own hometown. In St. Mark's words in the Gospel today, **"So he was not able to perform any mighty deed there, apart from curing a few sick people by laying His hands on them. He was amazed at their lack of faith."** I suspect it was not that the people lacked the will to have faith, it was that they couldn't bring themselves to have faith in someone so close.

So often, I think, we have the same problem as the people of Nazareth in today's Gospel. It's easy to believe in God when He's kept at a distance, and it's easy to love someone we don't see very often. We even have a proverb: **"Absence makes the heart grow fonder"** or the famous Charlie Brown saying: **"I love humanity...it's people I can't stand!"** But, sometimes, I think, the reason we see so little good going on around us in our country, in our own town, in our own neighborhood, or in our own family, is that we really look for it so faithlessly. **WE REALLY DON'T EXPECT** our children to be terrific. We really don't expect our parents to be understanding. We really don't think we'll see or hear great wisdom from the local valet parking attendant, a store clerk, a local teacher, an ex-convict, or our next door neighbor. The sad part of all this is that since we expect so little, we see so little. And we can go through our lives missing a lot of the good things and the good people around us. **We can even miss God Himself in our midst.** After all, the people of Nazareth didn't see Who Jesus really was. Sometimes we still take God for granted. We come late or carelessly to His Eucharist. We leave early because we have something more important to do than spend a few more minutes with God. We bend and twist God's teachings to suit our own convenience. And, sadly, the result is still the same as it was in Nazareth some 2000 years ago....Jesus could work no miracles there so much did their lack of faith distress Him.

Beginning today, maybe we can come to appreciate Jesus and His message a little bit more. Maybe we can recognize Him better in His Word, in the Eucharist, in His people, and in the good that He really tries to do around us and through us. We are, after all, on this 4th of July weekend, **ONE NATION UNDER GOD**, and we still have a chance to notice what Nazareth overlooked. Let's not miss it!

God bless you!

"Sometimes you just have to BEAR with me!"

15th Sunday in Ordinary Time - "B"

12 July 2009

FIRST READING: Amos 7:12-15
PSALM: Psalm 85:9-14
SECOND READING: Ephesians 1:3-14
GOSPEL: Mark 6:7-13

Jesus sends out the Twelve Apostles to preach and to teach and to share what they have received.

Another week in Paradise! Enjoyed some homemade tuna-macaroni salad, and a dessert called the **1000 Calorie Bar**! Believe me, it tasted so good that I know how it got its name! Got to see opening night of "**WEST SIDE STORY**" up in Las Vegas. My "illegitimate son" **(Relax, folks, it's a term of endearment!)** Eddie has the lead in it and he lost his voice the night before opening night. We both tried our favorite remedies....His remedy was to mix port wine with brandy and sip it. My remedy was an old homecure. I pulled out a jar of Vicks, boiled some water, mixed the Vicks with it. Then I covered his head with a towel and made him breathe it in. I told him if that didn't work, I was going to shove his head into the boiling water. It seemed to work ....so opening night was a huge success in front of 1100 people at Spring Mountain Ranch up in Vegas. Sometimes it's good to just pull out some of those old remedies that our Mom's used on us. They always seem to work.

A good friend of mine always tells me that he wants to send me some jokes, but he can never find any clean ones to share with me! Well, recently, he finally found something called **"Rules for Life"** and sent them to me. I liked them so much, I want to share a few of them with you. Sometimes we just need to remember what the R**ules for Life** REALLY are:

1. Never give yourself a haircut after three margaritas.

2. You need only two tools in life - WD-40 and duct tape.

   If it doesn't move and it should, use the WD-40.
   If it moves and it shouldn't, use the duct tape.

3. The two most essential phrases for a healthy relationship are:

   "I apologize" and **"You're right."**

4. Everyone seems normal until you get to know them.

5. When you make a mistake, make amends immediately.

   It's easier to eat crow when it's still warm.

6. The best advice your mother ever gave you was: "Go. You might meet somebody."

7. Learn to pick your battles: ask yourself, "Will this matter one year from now? How about one month? One week? One day?"

8. Work is good, but it's not all that important.

9. Living well really is the best revenge. Being miserable because of a bad or former relationship just may mean that the other person was right about you.

10. If you woke up today breathing, **CONGRATULATIONS!** You have another chance.

Today's Scripture readings give us some valuable and not so different insights into our lives as Catholic Christians in the world today. Think of them as good old home remedies for what ails us. Here are some **"rules for life"** from the readings today:

1. **GOD HAS GIVEN US EVERY SPIRITUAL BLESSING.** God has promised to be with us no matter what happens. He gives us **COURAGE** to face situations and people that are difficult. He gives us **STRENGTH** to carry on in the midst of problems. He gives us **JOY** to experience the goodness in the world around us.

2. In today's Gospel, Jesus tells His disciples not to take money, nor extra clothing, nor even food with them. These are important, indeed very important, but they are not the **MOST IMPORTANT** things in life. Wealth, abundance of possessions, even all-around good health are not the **ESSENTIAL MARKS OF A CHRISTIAN.**

3. Jesus sends us out into the world around us equipped with every **SPIRITUAL BLESSING.** If people are rejoicing on a good day, then we should share in their joy because it is something we can all be joyful about. If people are sorrowing over a death, a job loss, an illness, or whatever else might be causing sorrow, then we should be just as quick to share it with them and let them feel the comfort of our Faith and of our presence.

So what are the real rules for life? Use what God has given to you. Be generous and mindful of other people. Appreciate the great spiritual blessings you have received. Let Christ live in the world through you.

Oh, and maybe that one about WD-40 and duct tape is worth remembering.......Help those things and people that should be moving to move and grow in the way that God wants, and when things are whirling around for some people, help them to slow down and see the world as God sees it.

Spiritual WD-40 and spiritual duct tape may just be the most important tools God has given us to share.

God bless you!

16th Sunday in Ordinary Time - "B"

19 July 2009

FIRST READING: Jeremiah 23:1-6
PSALM: Psalm 23:1-6
SECOND READING: Ephesians 2:13-18
GOSPEL: Mark 6:30-34

Jesus is our Good Shepherd, the One Who guides and cares for us throughout our journey in life.

It's warming up a bit here in Paradise. Remember, it's not really **HOT** here until it stays above 100 for 24 hours straight! **That should be next week sometime!** I love the interesting things I learn and get to do here in Nevada. This week, Eddie's girlfriend, who is studying neuro-biology took Eddie into the lab with her. She was dissecting fruitflies because the fruitfly apparently has a brain very similar to the human brain. Eddie was amazed at this and was telling me all about it at home this week. It didn't seem all that surprising to me. I told Eddie that I've thought for months that he had the brain of a fruitfly! And I got to a Byzantine Catholic Church in Las Vegas for the Mount Carmel Novena this week. The priest called me up to the altar to join in the Mass and he put vestments on me that were about three sizes too small! For those unfamiliar with the Byzantine Catholic Church, it is one of about two dozen rites in our Catholic Church that differ from the Roman

(Latin) rite that we have here. They use a lot of incense and candles and singing. What would have taken us about 15 minutes took them about two hours! And there I was at the altar trying to not burst out of the tight vestments, and dodging the guy swinging the incense all around me! Speaking of dodging, I was at Spring Mountain State Park this week to see **"West Side Story"** again, and there were hundreds of dragonflies flying all around us at this outside theatre. The announcer told us not to worry about the dragonflies because as soon as it gets dark, the bats will come out to eat them! So I felt much better with bats flying all around my head! I was glad to get home to Laughlin! It really is Paradise.

One of the funniest comedy routines I have ever heard is Bill Cosby talking about how he would go to sleep as a little boy. He would turn off the light, and dive for the bed, and bury himself under the covers with only his nose sticking out so he could breathe. As he put it, there was something magical about covers that kept the monsters away. All of us probably went through that stage of being afraid of the dark, in fact, I still sleep with my head covered and only my nose exposed. When I was in college, my roommate described me asleep as looking like a **"500 year old nun!"**- probably way more than you ever wanted to know about me!

In today's Gospel, the Apostles return to Jesus and report to Him all they have done and all they have taught. I'm sure that many times in the course of their ministry, the Apostles did this - they came to Jesus to talk over their day. In today's Gospel, Jesus listens to them and then says to them, **"Come away by yourselves to a deserted place and rest awhile."** But I'm sure that there were other times when Jesus questioned them with things like, **"Why did you do that?" ..... "Why did you say that? ..... Why didn't you make time for that? ..... "Why didn't you go there?"**

It is obvious from the Gospels that Jesus made Himself totally available to all who sought Him. He never turned people away. He always made time for them. Even in today's Gospel, as Jesus and the Apostles try to get a little well-deserved rest, Jesus gives up His rest to teach the crowds.

We might do well to take a lesson from the Apostles and spend a little time each day talking over our day with Jesus. Before we jump or crawl into our bed, we might want to set aside some time to just report in to Jesus about what we have said and done throughout the day. Can you imagine the great wonders that could be worked in our lives if each one of us really tried each day to be accountable to Jesus for what we say and do? Can you even imagine how many good works would be accomplished, how many sick and needy people would be cared for and visited, how many lonely people would find listeners, how many unkind thoughts would remain forever unspoken, how many mean acts would never be done?

Reporting in to Jesus each night could change our whole lives, and the lives of those around us.

It's something to think about, each night, before we pull those covers up over our heads.

God bless you!

17th Sunday in Ordinary Time - "B"

26 July 2009

FIRST READING:2 Kings 4:42-44
PSALM: Psalm 145:10-11, 15-18
SECOND READING: Ephesians 4:1-6
GOSPEL: John 6:1-15

Jesus feeds a crowd of more than 5000 people with just a little bread and fish. It's no wonder that He is attracting a lot of attention!

Ah, another great week in Paradise! But what a tie-up on Route 95 this past Monday! Road was closed for nearly 12 hours, trucks were backed up for 16 miles in all directions. Fortunately, it got all cleared out for Tuesday so I could get up to Vegas for my day off. Had some amazing cheese enchiladas on Tuesday afternoon and then enjoyed a Palestinian meal of tabouli, humus, and falafel on Tuesday night. I then met some friends on Wednesday night for dinner at the oldest German restaurant in Las Vegas - Café Heidelburg - for chicken schnitzel smothered in mushrooms with spaetzle and red cabbage. Finished the week off with a homemade chicken dinner and an amazing pumpkin roll filled with cream cheese and walnuts.

The most interesting thing I got to do on Wednesday was to take a tour of the Las Vegas Athletic Clubs.

The senior VP comes to Mass at St. John's when he's visiting Laughlin and he asked me if I would like to see where he works. **I figured it was only fair since he has seen where I work!**So we met up on Wednesday and I got the grand tour of 3 of the clubs in Vegas. Mighty impressive.....the last time I had been in a gym was back in the 1990's in the Air Force. Trust me, these new facilities are much nicer! Impressive equipment, some of the biggest guys I've ever seen in my life, and even a 24 hour juice and snack bar! We might have to figure out how to get one of these here in Paradise!

There is probably no one who enjoys food more than I do. And I think it's a safe bet most of you enjoy food also. With that in mind, it's interesting to note that besides the Resurrection, the only miracle story contained in all four Gospels - Matthew, Mark, Luke, and John - is the story of Jesus multiplying the bread and fish to feed thousands of people. So even though we've heard the story many times before, it's something we all can be interested in each time we hear it.

And even though I know we've all heard the story before, I'd just like to point out two things about it today that we may not always have thought about when we've heard the story:

1. We should not fail to notice that Jesus always does **MORE THAN ENOUGH**. It would be miracle

enough for Jesus to feed 5000 people from just five small loaves of bread, **but there were twelve baskets of bread left over after the miracle**. I like to think that God works like that in our lives today. **He never does just barely enough.** He always gives us more than we need, more than we deserve, more than enough to show His love and care for us. So much more that we will be convinced that God really and truly cares about us even more than we ever imagined.

2. The miracle started with a little boy sharing his bread with Jesus. God can take the little we have on our own, and do great things with it. In this same vein, a priest, Anthony De Mello, tells this wonderful story: Paul had received a special gift from his rich brother. It was a beautiful new car - fully-loaded and ready to go. A few days later, when Paul came out of his office, a street kid was walking around the shiny new car, admiring it. **"Is this your car, mister?"** the kid asked. When he replied that it was and that his brother had given it to him as a gift, the boy said, **"You mean your brother gave it to you, and it didn't cost you anything? Free? For Nothing? Gosh, I wish..."** The boy hesitated, and Paul knew what he was about to say. He had heard it many times over the past few days. **He was going to wish he had a brother like that.**

But what the boy said shocked Paul."**I wish**", the boy said, "**I wish I could be a brother like that.**"

We can be a brother like that or a sister like that. All it takes is that we offer ourselves and what we have to God. All it takes is that we cease to worry about how little we have and begin instead to think about what it is we can offer to others, as the little boy in today's gospel story did by sharing his bread and fish with the multitude through Jesus.

God bless you!

Sharing a beer with my brother.

18th Sunday in Ordinary Time - "B"

2 August 2009

FIRST READING: Exodus 16:2-4, 12-15
PSALM: Psalm 78:3-4, 23-25, 54
SECOND READING: Ephesians 4:17, 20-24
GOSPEL: John6:24-35

Jesus is truly our Bread of life. He shares His own life with us through the Holy Eucharist.

What a nice warm week here in Paradise! We are so lucky to be living here in a vacation resort, and our visitors are so lucky to be able to come here and enjoy it with us. I feel like I'm on a permanent vacation! And this was a banner week for eating! Had some homemadegolumpke (stuffed cabbage), chicken with rice, and strawberry shortcake. Had a huge (and I do mean HUGE!) chicken sandwich up in Vegas at a place called the Hash House a Go-Go. Even took pictures of it! Some folks have pictures of their children, I have pictures of extra-special meals! Down here in Laughlin, I had a memorable meal overlooking our beautiful Colorado River at one of the casinos, and for dessert they served a basket made of almonds, sugar, honey and vanilla, and then filled it with vanilla ice cream. Trust me, there was not a speck left on the plate when I was finished! Several folks in the parish ended up with back problems this week, and I ended up being one of them. Have no idea what I did, but I plan on never doing it again! Right now I'm loaded up with enough pain-killers to sink a ship so I feel kind of like I'm floating a little. And you all look like you're kind of fuzzy and nice right now.

Despite my love for food, I am not a great chef, and sometimes when I try to fool around in the kitchen I can create some notable taste treats and some memorable culinary disasters. I have actually exploded a pressure-cooker, set fire to a toaster oven (who knew that the bacon on bacon-wrapped scallops contained grease that would catch fire?), and filled a microwave with foaming oatmeal. I've also learned that putting instant coffee into the coffee maker causes a problem. Apparently instant coffee isn't made to be used in that way. And of course, there was the memorable incident with the juicer which resulted in orange peels, pulp and juice being splattered all over the kitchen. (I guess I should have read the instructions which probably said something like **"Do not turn on until you have put the lid on."**) And sometimes I like unusual (my friends would say "disgusting") combinations of foods. For example, I enjoy eating pasta with no sauce, but only a few spoons of cottage cheese mixed in with it. And oatmeal with cheddar cheese sprinkled on top of it. Maybe it's just as well that I eat out a lot and that people send in some food to the rectory.

No matter what our particular culinary skill levels and no matter what our particular food preferences, I think it is a safe bet that we all enjoy food. So today's readings should catch our attention rather easily.

Today's readings speak of an important type of food - **BREAD**. The amazing thing about bread is that in virtually every society **BREAD** is a main food item. Many of us can't even imagine a meal without some form of bread. It is so basic to our lives.

In the Old Testament, when God wanted to show His people in the desert that He would sustain them throughout their journey, He gave them bread each day. Today's first reading from the Book of Exodus reminds us about this miraculous manna that God gave His people in the desert for those 40 years.

In the Gospel today, Jesus describes Himself as the **BREAD OF LIFE.** He is the source of our life. He is the most basic ingredient in living. Just as we can't imagine a meal without bread, so as Catholic Christians, we shouldn't be able to imagine life without Christ.

Is this really how we feel about Jesus? Is it this sense of longing and knowing we can't make it without Him that brings us to church each Sunday and makes us want to receive Him in Holy Communion? And if we are prevented from receiving

Communion because of some sinful actions in our lives, doesn't the desire to be able once again to receive Communion provide us with the incentive to make a good confession and be absolved of our sins, or take whatever steps are necessary to be reconciled with the Church? A meal without bread is unthinkable for most of us. Life without Christ should be even more unthinkable for us as Catholic Christians. Jesus said, **"I am the Bread of life. Whoever comes to Me will never hunger, and whoever believes in Me will never thirst."**

For the next several Sundays, the Gospels will be about Jesus as the true Bread of Life. His Real Presence in the Holy Eucharist under the appearances of bread and wine is one of the hallmarks of our Catholic beliefs. Whatever you're having for dinner tonight, when you pick up a piece of bread to go with your meal, think of Jesus Who comes to you here at church under the appearances of bread and wine. May we always appreciate His love for us and His presence in our lives.

God bless you!

"Can you see the resemblance between
Eddie and me?"

19th Sunday in Ordinary Time - "B"

9 August 2009

FIRST READING: 1 Kings 19:4-8
PSALM: Psalm 34:2-9
SECOND READING: Ephesians 4:30 - 5:2
GOSPEL: John 6:41-51

Just like God cared for the Prophet Elijah in the desert, so God continues to care for us today, feeding and nourishing us along the journey of life.

Another awesome week in Paradise! And the weather even cooled off a little. The Riverside celebrated its 43rd anniversary with champagne and cake on Monday. How cool is that!? And it was a great week for eating: Noodles and sauerkraut, ice cream pie, some amazing salads, and the best cauliflower I have ever had in my life! It was cooked, put in a blender with a little butter substitute, and came out like an awesome batch of mashed potatoes! And **"GOOD VIBRATIONS"** is back in town through Sunday night at the Riverside. They were here last year and they are still the best Beach Boys Tribute group I've ever seen! So I've been humming Beach Boys' songs all weekend! It just doesn't get any better than Laughlin!

When I'm not eating or going to shows, I like to play around on the computer. There are websites for everything these days. There's one for wait-ers called "**WAITER'S REVENGE**"where waiters and waitresses can post the most annoying things that customers in restaurants have done to them.....and what funny or disgusting things they have done to get even! It's worth checking out, but it may make you a little worried about eating out for awhile!

There are even some websites for preachers, and one lists some comments about sermons and preaching. I jotted down some comments from that site:

The definition of a good sermon: It should have a good beginning. It should have a good ending. And they should be as close together as possible.

A sermon should be modeled on a woman's dress: long enough to cover the subject, but short enough to be interesting.

A rule of thumb for preachers: If after ten minutes you haven't struck oil, stop boring!

A woman said, **"Father, that was a very good ser-mon**!" The priest said, **"Oh, I have to give the credit to the Holy Spirit."** And the woman replied, **"It wasn't THAT good!"**

A little child in the congregation noticed that before beginning his sermon each Sunday, the priest would bow his head for a moment. One Sunday after Mass, the child approached the priest and asked him why he did that. The priest responded to the child by saying **"Well, I'm just asking the Lord to help me preach a really good sermon."** To which the child innocently replied, **"Then how come He doesn't do it?"**

So, with that in mind, on to today's sermon.....

There once was a king who offered a prize to the artist who would paint the best picture of **PEACE**. Many artists tried. The king looked at all the pictures. But there were only two he really liked, and he had to choose between them. One picture was of a calm lake. The lake was a perfect mirror for peaceful towering mountains all around it. Overhead was a blue sky with fluffy white clouds. All who saw this picture thought it was a perfect picture of peace. The other picture too had mountains, but they were rugged and bare. Above was an angry sky, from which rain fell and in which lightning played. Down the side of the mountain tumbled a foaming waterfall. This did not look peaceful at all! But when the king looked closely, he saw behind the waterfall a tiny bush growing in a crack in the rock. In the bush a mother bird had build her nest. There, in the midst of the rush of angry water, sat the mother bird on her nest...in perfect peace.

Which picture do you think won the king's prize? The king chose the second picture. Do you know why? **"Because,"** explained the king, **"peace does**

not mean to be in a place where there is no noise, trouble or hard work. Peace means to be in the midst of all those things and still be calm in your heart. This is the real meaning of peace."

Today's readings remind us of the strength that God can give us in the midst of all that life can throw at us. In the First reading, Elijah was fleeing for his life because Queen Jezebel had sent her troops after him to kill him. God provided him with food and drink and gave him strength to complete his journey to safety on Mount Horeb. In Paul's letter to the Ephesians, we're told to imitate God Himself in getting rid of malice and anger, and in learning to live in kindness and compassion. And in the Gospel, Jesus reminds us that He is the living bread that came down from heaven. And He gives us this bread in the Holy Eucharist to give us strength for our journey through life wherever it might lead us.

The lessons for us are simple and obvious. Think of that picture of peace, realize your Faith gives you the ability to face whatever life throws at you, learn to depend on God more than anyone else and never give up on sharing your Faith with those around you in whatever ways you can. Remember: **"Peace does not mean to be in a place where there is no noise, trouble or hard work. Peace means to be in the midst of all those things, and still be calm in your heart. This is the real meaning of peace."**

God bless you!

Family Night Out!

20th Sunday in Ordinary Time - "B"

16 August 2009

FIRST READING: Proverbs 9:1-6
PSALM: Psalm 34:2-3, 10-15
SECOND READING: Ephesians 5:15-20
GOSPEL: John 6:51-58

Wisdom provides a banquet for us to share. Jesus gives us the true Banquet of life....His own Body and Blood.

Another awesome week in Paradise! And the food was plentiful! Several loaves of homemade bread, cream cheese squares, sticky buns, banana split bread, garlic mashed potatoes. Dinner with an old friend up in Las Vegas. And a whole shopping bag filled with Pittsburgh Steelers merchandise! I have to admit that the Steelers' fans give me stuff so I'm inclined to wear it and use it. But just for the record, I could wear socks from other teams if they happened to come my way. And a phone call from a friend in NJ telling me that it has been raining all week.That made me enjoy our sunshine even more!

I also got several great books this week! One was a Lithuanian cookbook. My nationality is Lithuanian and now I have a whole book of recipes from my heritage! All I need to do is find someone who wants to make some of them! Lithuanians have some great foods and beverages. One of my favorite is something called **VITITUS**. It is a winter-time drink which starts with 180 proof grain alcohol to which you then add cloves and cinnamon and honey and carroway seeds and allspice. Maybe next winter I'll whip up a batch for us. Also got 3 joke books from one of the parishioners - **THE WORLD'S GREATEST COLLECTION OF CHURCH JOKES, 777 GREAT CLEAN JOKES, and JOLLY JOKES FOR OLDER FOLKS.** I'm pretty sure you're going to be hearing some of them in the coming months, but here's a sample: **Did you hear about the hunter who had a close call last week? He saw some tracks and went over to look at them closely. That's when the train almost hit him.**

(I don't think I should reveal the name of the parishioner who gave me these books.)

When I think of books that are memorable, I always remember one book from my past - the **Baltimore Catechism**. From 1891 until 1963, it was the standard religion text in all Catholic schools and religious education programs. Just out of curiosity.... how many of you remember the Baltimore Catechism from your own youth? It was a very straight-forward presentation of what we Catholics believe, and the methodology was just as straight-forward. You memorized the questions and answers until you could say them in your sleep. Even today, many of those memorized questions and answers come back to us very easily. And we always answered in complete sentences. For example, see if you can remember the answers to these basic Baltimore Catechism questions:

Who made the world?

GOD MADE THE WORLD.

Who is God?

GOD IS THE CREATOR OF HEAVEN AND EARTH, AND OF ALL THINGS.

Where is God?

GOD IS EVERYWHERE.

Who made you?

GOD MADE ME.

Why did God make you?

GOD MADE ME TO KNOW HIM, TO LOVE HIM, AND TO SERVE HIM IN THIS WORLD, AND TO BE HAPPY WITH HIM FOREVER IN THE NEXT.

What is a sacrament?

A SACRAMENT IS AN OUTWARD SIGN INSTITUTED BY CHRIST TO GIVE GRACE.

We may not have understood everything, but we sure knew what we believed. For the past several Sundays, we've been hearing about the Bread of

Life, the life of Jesus Himself, in the Holy Eucharist. I thought it would be interesting to refresh ourselves on what the Baltimore Catechism taught us about this great sacrament. Questions 238 through 250 in the Catechism deal with the Holy Eucharist.

What is the Holy Eucharist?

THE HOLY EUCHARIST IS THE SACRAMENT WHICH CONTAINS THE BODY AND BLOOD, SOUL AND DIVINITY, OF OUR LORD JESUS CHRIST UNDER THE APPEARANCES OF BREAD AND WINE.

When did Christ institute the Holy Eucharist?

CHRIST INSTITUTED THE HOLY EUCHARIST AT THE LAST SUPPER, THE NIGHT BEFORE HE DIED.

Who were present when Our Lord instituted the Holy Eucharist?

WHEN OUR LORD INSTITUTED THE HOLY EUCHARIST THE TWELVE APOSTLES WERE PRESENT.

How did Our Lord institute the Holy Eucharist?

OUR LORD INSTITUTED THE HOLY EUCHARIST BY TAKING BREAD, BLESSING, BREAKING, AND GIVING TO HIS APOSTLES, SAYING: "Take ye and eat. This is My body"; and then by taking the cup of wine, blessing and giving it, saying to them: "Drink ye all of this. This is My blood which shall be shed for the remission of sins. Do this for a commemoration of Me."

What happened when Our Lord said "This is My body; this is My blood?"

WHEN OUR LORD SAID "THIS IS MY BODY" THE SUBSTANCE OF THE BREAD WAS CHANGED INTO THE SUBSTANCE OF HIS BODY; WHEN HE SAID "THIS IS MY BLOOD," THE SUBSTANCE OF THE WINE WAS CHANGED INTO THE SUBSTANCE OF HIS BLOOD.

Did anything remain of the bread and wine after their substance had been changed into the substance of the body and blood of Our Lord?

AFTER THE SUBSTANCE OF THE BREAD AND WINE HAD BEEN CHANGED INTO THE SUBSTANCE OF THE BODY AND BLOOD OF OUR LORD THERE REMAINED ONLY THE APPEARANCES OF BREAD AND WINE.

What do we mean by the appearances of bread and wine?

BY THE APPEARANCES OF BREAD AND WINE WE MEAN THE FIGURE, THE COLOR, THE TASTE, AND WHATEVER APPEARS TO THE SENSES.

Does this change of bread and wine into the body and blood of Christ continue to be made in the Church?

THIS CHANGE OF BREAD AND WINE INTO THE BODY AND BLOOD OF CHRIST CONTINUES TO BE MADE IN THE CHURCH BY JESUS CHRIST THROUGH THE MINISTRY OF HIS PRIESTS.

How do the priests exercise this power of changing bread and wine into the body and blood of Christ?

THE PRIESTS EXERCISE THIS POWER OF CHANGING BREAD AND WINE INTO THE BODY AND BLOOD OF CHRIST THROUGH THE WORDS OF CONSECRATION IN THE MASS, WHICH ARE THE WORDS OF CHRIST: THIS IS MY BODY; THIS IS MY BLOOD.

Every time we come to Mass, we are sharing in this great sacrament. Take a little time today and just try to appreciate how fortunate we are that God wants to share His own life with us. "I am the living bread that came down from heaven, whoever eats this bread will live forever; and the bread that I will give is my flesh for the life of the world.....Whoever eats my flesh and drinks my blood has eternal life, and I will raise him on the last day."

All the other food we eat, and all the other drinks we drink, somehow are assimilated into our bodies and contribute to our earthly life. But the Holy Eucharist has the power to assimilate us into God's own life and contribute to our eternal life. It's a miracle, it's a grace, it's a wonder, it's a gift God offers to us here at Mass. I hope we never ever forget how fortunate we are to be here. The lessons we learned from that old Baltimore Catechism should keep us on the right track. It's basic and straightforward like the opening questions. Let's see if we remember them:

Who made you?

GOD MADE ME.

Why did God make you?

GOD MADE ME TO KNOW HIM, TO LOVE HIM AND TO SERVE HIM IN THIS WORLD, AND TO BE HAPPY WITH HIM IN THE NEXT.

Don't ever forget who you are, and where you're heading!

God bless you!

Good Times! Good people!

21st Sunday in Ordinary Time - "B"

23 August 2009

FIRST READING: Joshua 24:1-2a, 15-17, 18b
PSALM: Psalm 34:2-3, 16-23
SECOND READING: Ephesians 5:21-32
GOSPEL: John 6:60-69

To whom could we ever go, if we were to walk away from the Lord? It's an important choice for each one to make.

What a great week in Paradise! Some awesome tuna salad, some banana chocolate cream cake, and a Javanese Dinner. In case you're wondering what that is, it's like a buffet, but you layer everything on top of everything else and build a **"mountain"** of food! It was hard to choose the items, but I built a base from white rice, then added Chinese noodles, a little bit of chicken, celery, onions, pineapple, coconut, sliced almonds, cheddar cheese and then some chicken/peanut sauce. **AWESOME!** Makes me want to visit Java!

But the best part of this week was my vacation. For five days from Sunday afternoon until Thursday morning, I was up in Las Vegas at the **MAGIC LIVE** gathering. 1000 magicians from around the world.....and me! Got to hang out with some of the greats in the world of magic like Johnny Thompson. He's almost 90 years old and I used to watch him when I was a kid on TV when he did his act as **"The Great Tomsoni"**. He did his act once again for us.... it was a moment in history! And Mervyn Roy was there....also well up in years....you may remember him from the 1950's and 1960's as **"Mr. Electric"** on TV. And the current greats were there too.....Jeff McBride, Lance Burton, Mac King, Steve Wyrick, Andre Kole, Tim Kole, Ed Alonzo, Kevin James, Losander, Dirk Arthur, Murray SawChuck, David Blaine, and Franz Harary (to name a few). Franz Harary is coming to the Riverside in September so I'll be at several of his shows. I mentioned to him that we share the showroom at the Riverside, so if he is nice to me, I'll make sure the Saturday evening Mass ends in time for him to set up.....otherwise.....we're staying! There was magic everywhere, and I was getting to bed about 3AM each night (morning). **For a magic lover like me, it was better than meeting the pope!**

One of my friends there who is a magician had a new poster designed for him. He's a talented young guy so I asked him to autograph a copy for me and date it. I told him that I wanted the date on it so **"50 years from now when I'm going through my things, I can look back and remember when I got it."** He looked at me weirdly and said, **"50 years from now!?....you mean when I'M GOING THROUGH YOUR THINGS after you're gone!"** I love my friends!

We got to choose elective classes and I went to the one on comedy writing (figure I can use that in my sermons) and on creativity. It was hard to choose from all the options offered. In the one on creativity, they gave each one of us a paperclip and asked us to shout out things we could do with a paperclip other than clip papers together. MAKE AN EARRING, CLEAN YOUR EAR, CLEAN THE LINT OUT OF YOUR BELLYBUTTON, PICK A LOCK. Then one guy yelled out **"make a circle out of it and use it as an engagement ring."** From across the room, a young woman yelled out, **"You're still single, aren't you?....and you always will be!"**

You may have noticed that our Second Reading today is a famous reading about husbands and wives. I remember a wonderful story about a group of couples at a marriage enrichment session. The speaker told the couples that they should know and remember all the little important things about their spouses. For example, he said, all of you husbands should know your wife's favorite flower. John turned to his wife, Mary, and gently held her hand, and whispered to her, **"I know your favorite flower."** Mary was touched, and almost shedding a tiny tear of joy, and then John continued, **"It's Pillsbury, isn't it." Perhaps not a good choice on his part.**

There's a wonderful old story about a man who hated making choices. Every time he had to make a choice, he got really nervous. And he feared making the wrong choice. If he came to a toll booth, he had to pick which line...and it usually ended up being the slowest one. If he got on line in the supermarket, he ended up behind the person who counted out the pennies one-by-one to pay the clerk. He just hated having to make choices even in a restaurant on a menu. Well, one day he was out hiking and he slipped and fell off the side of the cliff, but he was able to grab hold of a branch and there he was hanging over the edge, clutching on to the one thin branch. He was in a serious panic! So he decided to pray. And he prayed to his favorite saint, Saint Francis. **"St. Francis,"** he cried out, **"Please save me!"** And he heard a voice from heaven which said, **"Do you want St. Francis of Assisi or St. Francis Xavier?"**

Today's readings have one thing in common - they remind us of the importance of making choices in our lives. And to be honest, most of us don't like making choices. Because to make a choice means we have to eliminate something. That's why people stare at menus in restaurants for a very long time trying to choose something to eat. They don't like coming to the moment of decision. We all have friends like that! The whole table is starving because they're not ready yet to make a choice!   But life is full of choices and today's readings remind us of some of the choices that must be made in our lives.

In the first reading from the Book of Joshua, Joshua insists that the people must make a choice to serve God or not. And he is clear about the choice he himself has made: **"As for me and my household, we will serve the Lord."** Let's face it....we're either going to serve the Lord or we're not. Oh we may not always succeed, but if we're honest with ourselves, we have to make a choice that we are going to try to serve the Lord to be best of our abilities.

In the second reading from St. Paul's Letter to the Ephesians, all of us are asked to choose to be subordinate to one another, to actually put service to others (not only husbands and wives) ahead of our own self-interest. If you read Ephesians carefully, it's not only husbands and wives who need to be in a right relationship with each other, it's all of us. That is definitely a tough choice to make and to live out. It is really hard to put another person first, but it is what we are called to do.

And in the Gospel, Jesus, Who has been describing Himself as the Bread of Life, asks His disciples to choose to stay with Him or to leave. He doesn't sugarcoat it, or say that He will bend His teaching to make it easier for them. He just tells them they have to make a choice to follow Him or not.   **Life involves choices.**

Some choices are of limited importance like what to eat for dinner or which shirt to wear. Some choices are more important like what type of education to pursue or what kind of a job to seek. Other choices are more significant like whom to marry. And still other choices are immensely important like being faithful to the Lord or not.

This weekend, as you choose which TV shows to watch or which foods to eat for dinner, think about the really important choices that we need to make in our lives.

Can we honestly say with Joshua, **"As for me and my household, we will serve the Lord"?**

Can we honestly say with St. Paul that we will try to be subordinate to one another, to put the good of others even ahead of our own interests?

Can we honestly answer Jesus as Peter did: **"Master, to whom shall we go? You have the worlds of eternal life. We have come to believe and are convinced that You are the Holy One of God."**

These are important choices. Choices that have eternal consequences. Choices that must be made.

May God always help us to make the right choices throughout our lives.

One of the choices I made at **MAGIC LIVE** involved learning to make some things magically appear. Like taking a simple napkin, and with a few twists and turns, making something beautiful from it. Maybe it's a good reminder for us today that we can all make our lives something beautiful for God with a little bit of well-placed effort. And the choices we make definitely affect the life we create for ourselves and for those around us.

God bless you!

More Good Times! More Good People! And One Live Snake!

22nd Sunday in Ordinary Time - "B"

30 August 2009

FIRST READING: Deuteronomy 4:1-2, 6-8
PSALM: Psalm 15:2-5
SECOND READING: James 1:17-18, 21b-22, 27
GOSPEL: Mark 7:1-8, 14-15, 21-23

The fullness of true life comes to us by our observance of the Lord's commands to us. There is no other way.

Another awesome week in Paradise. We hit 117 degrees one day, but it's a dry heat. Enjoyed some amazing chocolate fruitcake, and balanced it with some good fresh fruit this week. Had six sets of visitors in the area from back on the East Coast, so I had fun playing tourguide for them in Laughlin and in Vegas. Got to see some magic shows, went hiking in Red Rock Canyon, and got practically no sleep all week long. That's kind of becoming my tradition when I'm up in Vegas.....I'm having too much fun to even think about sleeping! It's been a great week!

I love hearing about family traditions, things people do on certain days or during certain events. Whenever someone comes to visit me out here, I always make sure I take them to walk along our beautiful River Walk. As you walk along, you can enjoy the amazing beauty of our Colorado River, and see all the ducks and the fish in the crystal clear water. And did you know that if you go out in the evening at one place, you can watch the cutest raccoons and one huge skunk play along the banks of the river as the tourists throw them scraps of food! I just keep hoping they don't accidently aggravate that skunk!

I once heard about an old family tradition that was truly amazing. Little Jimmy had heard from his grandma some amazing stories about an amazing family tradition. It seems his father, his grandfather, and his great-grandfather had all been able to walk on water on their 21st birthday back in Minnesota. On that day, they would walk across the lake to the boat club for their first legal drink of alcohol. So when Jimmy's 21st birthday came around, he and his pal, Joey, took a boat out to the middle of the lake. Jimmy stepped out of the boat, and sank like a stone! He nearly drowned, but Joey was able to pull him back into the boat to safety. Furious and confused, Jimmy went to see his grandmother. **"Grandma,"** he asked, **"it's my 21st birthday, so why can't I walk across the lake like my father, his father, and his father before him?"** Granny looked into Jimmy's eyes with a broad smile and said, **"Because your father, your grandfather, and your great-grandfather were born in January when the lake is frozen, and YOU WERE BORN IN AUGUST!"** Some traditions have to be thought about and investigated.

One of my traditions is that I love going through old papers and old notes I've written. This week, I found a sermon I preached back in New Jersey 6 years ago when I had returned from a trip out here to Nevada. I thought you might find it interesting what I had said 6 years before I moved out here on this very same Sunday. And since I've had practically no sleep this week, this is probably a better sermon than one I would have written in my sleep-deprived state!

Here's what I said six years ago on this very same Sunday.....

I'm so glad that I was able to make my annual summer trek out to my favorite place - Las Vegas - for the past few weeks. Las Vegas is one of the fastest growing regions of our nation and one of the fastest growing centers of Catholic population too. I thought I'd tell you a little about the churches of Las Vegas today.

The Shrine of the Holy Redeemer is right in the main casino section of Las Vegas. It seats over 2200 people (and is already too small), and is truly beautiful. Somewhat unusually, it has a full-sized gift shop for the tourists and even accepts credit cards for donations!

The Guardian Angel Cathedral sits right across the street from the Stardust Hotel/Casino. It has some magnificent mosaics. It claims that 75% of the people on a given Sunday are tourists, and 10% of the collection is in various casino tokens! In fact, each Monday, one of the priests makes a "casino run" cashing in all the tokens at the various casinos. (And he is **NOT** known as the chip-monk!). He is probably the only one to come out of a casino with as much money as he brings in! The Saturday Mass at the Cathedral is at 2:30 P.M. so the tourists can easily make it to dinner and to the evening shows.

Our Lady of Las Vegas Church has the most interesting sign over the holy water fonts. It reads **"Please do not throw coins and chips into the holy water for good luck."**

My personal favorite is St. John the Baptist Catholic Mission in Laughlin, Nevada, They get about 1500 people for the Masses on the weekends. But they have no permanent church building so all the Masses are in the casino showroom at the Riverside Casino. So the backdrop for Mass is whatever the current show happens to be! I love saying Mass there! One year it was a Harley-Davidson themed show; one year, it was the Bottom's Up Revue! Once it was a SKY VODKA themed show! And once I had the Budweiser Girls. Sometimes it is hard to hold people's attention there! (I have pictures to prove it!)

They are trying to raise money to build a church so they sell little glass fish after each Mass on Sunday since the town is right on the Colorado River. I have done many things in my life, but that was the first time I had ever sold fish after Sunday Mass!

Back here at home, or in the excitement of Las Vegas, or in the wilds of Nevada, or even in the casino showroom in Laughlin, Catholics gather on Sunday to hear the Word of the Lord and to worship His Presence in His Body and Blood in the Holy Eucharist. Wherever we are, God calls us together in His Presence. This is truly a blessing - that we can be together with others who share our Faith every week of our lives no matter where we are.

In today's First Reading, Moses tells the people they are blessed because God has given them His laws. God actually allows them to know what he expects of them! You and I share in that same blessing! The Commandments are not burdens on us; they are God showing His mercy and kindness to us by allowing us the privilege of knowing right from wrong. I wonder if we ever think of the Commandments as such a blessing? I hope we do!

And St. James reminds us in the Second Reading that we are expected to act on God's word, not just listen to it. Because we know the difference between right and wrong, we are supposed to act differently from those who don't!

And finally, in the Gospel today, Jesus tells us that **"evils come from within and they defile us"**. We are all called to look into our hearts and to clean out anything that leads us to evil, to get rid of evil thoughts, unchastity, theft, murder, adultery, greed, malice, deceit, licentiousness, envy, blasphemy, arrogance, folly. We are called to make sure our thinking and our acting are in conformity with God's eternal laws, and not just in line with the current way of thinking in the world, or the easy way out.

Next weekend is Labor Day Weekend, the unofficial end of summer and the beginning of a new start for many of us in school or at work. Whether we're in the bright lights of Las Vegas, in the casino-church in Laughlin, the wilds of Nevada or at our own home parish, God is giving us a new opportunity this week to draw ourselves closer to Him.

I hope the Summer of 2009 has been a good one for you, and I hope that the coming months will be even better as we join ourselves more closely with the Lord.

God loves us so very much! It's exciting even to think about it!

God bless you!

Preston, Mike, Andrew, Charlie, Paul and Me!

23rd Sunday in Ordinary Time - "B"

6 September 2009

FIRST READING:Isaiah 35:4-7a
PSALM: Psalm 146:6-10
SECOND READING: James 2:1-5
GOSPEL: Mark 7:31-37

The Lord Jesus helps a deaf man by restoring his sense of hearing and opening him up to the world around him.

Another great week in Paradise, with a surprising amount of rain and thunder and lightning. I had some visitors from New Jersey, so I suspect they brought the weather with them. Enjoyed going up to Vegas with them to see **THE LION KING** this week. What a great show! And I thoroughly enjoyed some tasty seafood soup, cinnamon crumb cake, wild huckleberry chocolate candy, Rice Krispie squares, and apple-cinnamon cobbler. My "illegitimate son" (Relax, folks, it's a term of endearment!) Eddie is auditioning with Cirque du Soleil as a young Elvis for their new show. He had to make a DVD of himself doing an Elvis monologue and then had to lip-sync Elvis doing **"You Ain't Nothing But a Hound Dog"** like Elvis did it on the Milton Berle show in 1963. So I got to sit through a few versions of **"You Ain't Nothing But a Hound Dog"** watching Eddie shake his hips around the living room, and then, because Eddie is

25, I had to explain to Eddie who Milton Berle was! Just one of the joys of being older than my friends and family!

An old man is talking to the family doctor, **"Doctor, I think my wife if going deaf."** The doctor answers, **"Well, here's a little something you can try on her to test her hearing. Stand some distance away from her without facing her and ask her a question. If she doesn't answer, move a little closer and ask again. Keep repeating this until she answers. Then you'll be able to tell just how hard-of- hearing she really is."** The man goes home and tries it out. He walks in the door and asks, **"Honey, what's for dinner?"** He doesn't hear an answer, so he moves closer to her, **"Honey, what's for dinner?"**. Still he gets no answer. He repeats this several times until he's standing just one foot away from her. Finally, she answers, **"For the 11ᵗʰ time, I said we're having meatloaf!"**

Another old gentleman had serious hearing problems for a number of years. He went to the doctor and the doctor was able to have him fitted with a set of hearing aids that allowed him to hear 100%. He went back to the doctor a month later for a check-up, and the doctor said, **"Your hearing is perfect. Your family must be really pleased that you can hear again."** The gentleman replied, **"Oh, I haven't told my family yet. I just sit around and listen to their conversations. I've changed my will three times already!"**

Hearing is one of our five senses that is so important to us. We depend on it throughout our lives. In fact, we even have a special ceremony connected with it in every baptism ceremony. Near the end of the ceremony, the priest places his hands on the baby's ears and runs his finger along the baby's mouth as he prays, **"May the Lord Jesus Who made the deaf hear and the dumb speak soon touch your ears to hear His word and your mouth to speak His praises."** That prayer and the actions associated with it are taken directly from today's Gospel. They are repeated at every baptism. They are done to every one of us.

As infants, we had no idea what was going on. Maybe now we can reflect a little on what happened. The man in today's Gospel had difficulty speaking and he was deaf. Jesus' action is deliberate and direct. He touches him and says **"Be opened!"**

Each of us here today is, in one way or another, just as handicapped or challenged as that man. We either don't hear the needs of people around us, or we hear them in a garbled way. We often are so busy in our noisy, cell-phone infested world, that we don't take the time or effort to hear the message of God in our lives. And we don't often speak the praises of God, or say the words of praise or correction that need to be said in our families, our homes, our places of work or education. We are, each one of us, somewhat closed into our own little world.

As we celebrate Mass this weekend, perhaps it would be a good idea to try to imagine Jesus Himself touching us and opening our ears to hear the needs of our neighbors and of our world, and opening our mouths to say what needs to be said in praise or in correction. It is important that we be opened. Remember what was said to each one of us on the day of our baptism: **"May the Lord Jesus Who made the deaf hear and the dumb speak soon touch your ears to hear His word and your mouth to speak His praises."** If it hasn't happened enough yet, may it happen very soon in all of our lives.

Besides God's word, one of the things we need to hear and remember is our own history. Friday, September 11th, marks the 8th Anniversary of the Islamic terrorist attacks on the United States of America. On that fateful morning, 19 male followers of Islam hijacked four commercial passenger jetliners. Each team of hijackers included a trained pilot. **American Airlines Flight 11** and **United Airlines Flight 175** crashed into the World Trade Center towers in New York City at 8:46 A.M. and 9:02 A.M. respectively. **American Airlines Flight 77** crashed into the Pentagon in Washington D.C. at 9:37 A.M. The fourth plane, **United Airlines Flight 93** crashed into a field near Shanksville, Pennsylvania, at 10:03 A.M. It is believed that passengers and crew members attempted to retake control of the plane which, it is believed, was planned to be crashed into the United States Capital in Washington, D.C. **Nearly 3000 people died as a direct result of this horrendous display of evil.**

Eight years later, we remember those who lost their lives because of these terrorist attacks. We pray for their families and friends whose lives were shattered. We pray for those who gave their lives in the rescue and recovery efforts. And we pray for the men and women of our Armed Services who today are fighting the war against terror at home and around the world. May God bless them, and us, as we fight against the powers of evil.

We need to hear God's words of comfort and strength as we remember this tragic anniversary. And we need to know God is with us enabling us to remember the past, to navigate the present, and to prepare for the future. We need to be open to the power and influence of God every day of our lives. Jesus' words **"Be opened"** are addressed to each one of us today and every day of our lives. We need to always listen to what God wants us to hear.

God bless you!

"Yes, John and I are eating Deep-fried Twinkies!"

24th Sunday in Ordinary Time - "B"

13 September 2009

FIRST READING: Isaiah 50:4-9a
PSALM: Psalm 116: 1-6, 8-9
SECOND READING: James 2:14-18
GOSPEL: Mark 8:27-35

Jesus asks His disciples some very important questions, questions which demand an answer from them.....and from us.

Another amazing week in Paradise! Chocolate-covered macadamia nuts, Filipino cheese and bacon buns, garlic mashed potatoes, chicken and rice casserole, and KUGEL (a Lithuanian potato and bacon pie). Had lunch with Fr. Peter across the river and got a tour of his new church building. What a beautiful structure! As we were coming out wearing our white hardhats, two workman approached Fr. Peter and asked if he knew where the emergency shut-off is for the irrigation system. He said he would be right with them, but they kept persisting, so I said, **"I think they are not just asking an academic question....I think they really need to know where the emergency shut-off is right now!"** And so they did! And the crisis was averted. I guess we were just in the right place at the right time.

And on Wednesday night, I was definitely in the right place at the right time. I was up in Las Vegas and I had read that Mayor Oscar Goodman and his wife Carolyn would be celebrating their 47th wedding anniversary at a special ceremony on Fremont Street. Now no one loves Las Vegas as much as Mayor Goodman, although I do think I come a close 2nd in loving Las Vegas! So I'm standing there in the crowd watching the lucky invited guests take their seats in a special fenced-off area. They are being served glasses of punch and special appetizers by tuxedoed waiters while we stood at a distance, outside the fenced off area, just looking in. All of a sudden, about 10 minutes before the event began, one of the staff comes up to me and says, **"Would you like to join us inside for the ceremony?"** She didn't have to ask me twice! I practically leaped over the fence! And there I was sitting with all the dignitaries eating little watermelon hearts with cheese on them, and some bruschetta, and drinking punch. An Elvis impersonator did the vow renewal (and did quite a good job of it, I might add! I might have to think of that as a possible career when I eventually retire!), and then Marilyn Monroe (okay, a look-alike) leaped out of a cake, and the Rat Pack appeared on the stage singing a few numbers, and then Zowie Bowie did a few more numbers. Then, just when I thought it was all over, they served me chocolate-covered strawberries and little pieces of anniversary cake, dipped in white chocolate and crowned with a fresh raspberry! Ah, it was good to be there! Right place, right time!

In today's Gospel, the disciples of Jesus find them-selves in the right place at the right time for Jesus to ask them a very important question.....actually two questions. **"Who do people say that I am?"** and **"Who do you say that I am?"** Jesus knew that there would be a difference in their answers. The people saw Jesus as just another one of the prophets, but the disciples saw Jesus as something (Someone) more than any of the prophets. **"You are the Christ."**

That's why Jesus is pressing His original followers, and us, with that same challenging question in today's Gospel - **"Who do you say that I am?"** A lot depends on how we answer.

If Jesus is really the Christ.....If Jesus really is Our God and Our Savior, that would change everything for us. Do you think we'd be careless about coming tochurch each week if we really believed God was here? Do you think we'd have our children bap-tized, but then never bring them to church until their First Communion if we really believed in Jesus? Do you think we'd send our kids to Catholic school or Religious Education classes and then never make it a family priority to come to church on Sunday if we really believed in Jesus? If we really believed, then our actions would show it. We would try to follow what Jesus teaches because He is Our God and Our Savior.

And Jesus takes us even further along the path of being His disciples by reminding us that it's one thing to say the right words, but it's something else to live them out each day, each month, each year. In today's Gospel, the disciples knew how to say the right words **("You are the Christ!")**, but when it came to understanding what that belief would cost them - the self-denial, the suffering, the reality of giving their lives over to the Lord - they didn't have a clue. They just didn't get it! And Jesus had to explain one more time that being His follower wasn't always going to be easy. Sometime the disciples would be hurt because they had to choose to do what was right, not what was convenient.

Sometimes, you and I can know the right words, but we neglect the actions that must follow them. We can be like Peter who wanted to acknowledge Jesus as the Messiah, but then wanted to go on doing what he did before, doing his own will and not what the Lord might require. If Jesus is Our God and Our Savior as we say He is, then shouldn't He have some control over our actions and lives? For those of us who come on Sunday, what we say here is great, but what we do the rest of the week is just as significant. If our actions on Monday match our words on Sunday, fine; if not, we need to make some changes.

So here we are, in the right place at the right time, for Jesus to ask us that challenging question, **"Who do you say that I am?"**

The way we answer makes all the difference in the world, because it will determine how we act today and during the week.

God bless you!

25th Sunday in Ordinary Time - "B"

20 September 2009

FIRST READING: Wisdom 2:12, 17-20
PSALM: Psalm 54:3-6, 8
SECOND READING: James 3:16-4:3
GOSPEL: Mark 9:30-37

Jesus places a little child in front of His disciples and He tells them that they need to learn to be more like little children in their approach to life.

Another Week here in Paradise! And now I've got a sign to prove it! One of our parish families picked this up for me on vacation. We really do live in an amazing place! And to make it even more amazing, we've got a **magic show** in town this week at the Riverside! And you know how much I love magic! I was there on Friday night, will be there on Saturday night, and will be back yet again on Sunday night. Hey, you can never have **TOO MUCH** magic in your life! Two friends of mine, Franz Harary and Murray SawChuck do some truly amazing things on stage. And I'm thinking of letting my hair grow like theirs! In fact, Murray will be with us for one of our Masses today. It's a deal we have.....I come to see him work, and he comes to see me work. It's just another amazing day here in Paradise!

And football season has started.....and the rivalry is growing intense. I've been given **Chicago Bears' socks** and **Green Bay Packers' socks** to add to my drawerful of **Pittsburgh Steelers' socks**. I had an interesting conversation with my brother Michael (who is an avid Steelers' fan). I told him about getting the Bears' socks and suggested I might wear them some weekend. He told me **NEVER** to wear them! When I protested, he told me I could wear them during the week, but **NEVER** on a game weekend. He finally told me **"Just don't ever wear Bears' socks on a Sunday! I thought we had you converted!"** I said, **"Well, just maybe I like bears!"** And he responded, **"Well, just maybe you should go live in the woods!"** Another Steelers' fan told me I would get a toe jam and green fungus if I dared to ever wear the **Green Bay Packers' socks**. I think I'm going to start wearing boots so no one can tell which socks I have on anyway!

After the way-too-serious discussions of football, I kind of like to relax and think about some much-less-serious comments made by children. Here are a few to think about:

Melanie (Age 5) asked her Grandmother how old she was. Grandma replied that she was so old she didn't remember any more. Melanie said, **"If you don't remember, you just look in the back of your underwear. See, mine say five to six."**

Tammy (Age 5) was with her mother when they met an elderly, rather wrinkled woman her mother knew. Tammy looked at her for awhile and then asked, **"Why doesn't your skin fit your face?"**

One particular Sunday, the priest began his sermon, **"Dear Lord,"** he said with his arms extended toward heaven and a rapturous look on his face, **"Without You, we are but dust."** He would have continued but a little girl in the congregation who was paying close attention leaned over to her mother and said (very loudly), **"Mom, what is butt dust?"**

A Sunday school teacher was bringing her class over to church. She asked them **"Why is it necessary to be quiet in church?"** And one bright young girl responded, **"Because people are sleeping!"**

A father was at the beach with his children when his four-year-old son ran up to him, grabbed his hand, and led him to the shore where a seagull lay dead in the sand. **"Daddy, what happened to him?"** the son asked. **"He died and went to heaven"**, the Dad replied. The boy thought for a minute and then said,,**"Did God throw him back down?"**

A wife invited some people to dinner. At the table, she turned to their six-year-old daughter and said, **"Would you like to say the blessing?"** The little girl replied, **"I wouldn't know what to say."** So the mother answered, **"Just say what you hear Mommy say."**

And the little girl bowed her head and said, **"Lord, why on earth did I invite all these people to dinner!"**

I want to say something about children today in the sermon.

Several times in the Gospels, it is recorded that Jesus put a little child in front of the group of His disciples. He then said to then **"THIS IS WHAT I WANT YOU TO BE LIKE!"** Jesus does that today in the reading from St. Mark's Gospel. We all want to be **YOUNG** like children. We all want to have the incredible **ENERGY** of children. We all like to get the **ATTENTION** that children get from their parents. We all like a lot of things we see in children.

But most of us don't approach life like children. For a child, everything is **NEW**, everything is **EXCITING**. Even stuffed animals take on a life of their own in the eyes of a child. There is a **FIRST TIME** a child crawls, a **FIRST TIME** a child walks, a **FIRST TIME** a child talks, a **FIRST TIME** a child eats carrots, sees a snowflake, goes to a picnic. A child is always experiencing something new! A child is always learning some new things.

BUT WHAT HAPPENS TO US WHEN WE GROW UP? We adults so often become really **OLD** before our time because we cease to see life through the eyes of a child. We actually think we have seen it all, heard it all, done it all, know it all. You've all heard that awful expression **"Been there, done that, sent**

postcards!" For some sad adults, life becomes just a dull replay. We learn **FEAR**, we learn **MISTRUST**, we learn **PREJUDICE**. Children on the other hand are not generally fearful, they tend to trust everyone, and they couldn't even spell "prejudice" much less practice it!

Perhaps the best lesson we could take from today's Gospel is to try to view life, approach life and live life as a child - without FEAR, with TRUST, without PREJUDICE. We are always capable of learning and experiencing new things. **The child in each of us can learn to live again!**

We may no longer be young in age. We may not have all the energy of a little child anymore. But all of us can learn to once again meet each day with a child's sense of WONDER and AWE and ANTICIPATION.

Hey, it may seem foolish to think of the way a child views life, but I hope all of you have at least some memories of your childhood. It was a time when life was less-cluttered, when faith in God seemed so natural, when the world seemed so friendly, wonderful and exciting. Yes, the child in each one of us wants to live again and can learn to live again. And the world can become a very different place when seen through the eyes of a trusting child.

This week, remember that we are all children of God, that Jesus invites us to recapture our youth, and to see the magic all around us in the world. The child in me invites the child in you to take another look at life. I think you might like what you see.

God bless you!

"Getting in shape with Thom and Jason"

26th Sunday in Ordinary Time - "B"

27 September 2009

FIRST READING: Numbers 11:25-29
PSALM: Psalm 19:8, 10, 12-14
SECOND READING: James 5:1-6
GOSPEL: Mark 9:38-43, 45, 47-48

Sometimes we place too many limits on God's power. After all, God can choose anyone He wishes to carry out His will.

No Father Charlie sermon in Laughlin this weekend because Father Charlie was back on the East Coast for a visit to New Jersey and to officiate at the Andrew Gerstmayr and Andrea Manfredonia wedding in New York State.

27th Sunday in Ordinary Time - "B"

4 October 2009

FIRST READING: Genesis 2:18-24
PSALM: Psalm 128:1-6
SECOND READING: Hebrews 2:9-11
GOSPEL: Mark 10:2-16

God's plan for marriage is a permanent plan. Every wedding celebrates the union of a husband and wife as a permanent and loving relationship.

Wow! It sure is great to be back in Paradise! I was away for 9 days.....and I don't ever want to do that again! Oh, I had a lot of fun....I went back to the East Coast to visit my Aunt in a nursing home in North Carolina, then up to Lake George, NY, to officiate at a wedding for two friends (Andrew and Andrea), and then back to NJ to spend some time with some of my old parishioners. But it just wasn't Paradise back there! It was cold (40 degrees at night!) And it rained for a few of the days I was there. And my friend doesn't turn on the heat until November.....so there I was freezing under a sheet, blanket, down comforter, and anything else I could pile on at night. And it was a twin bed.....so when I went to turn over.....it was a disaster! And my Aunt is in a nursing home with the beginnings of alzheimer's like my Mom (her sister) had. She asked me how old I was, and when I told her I was 61, she said **"How'd you get to be such an old man?"** The wedding up in Lake George was awesome, and I wore my new western suit and black boots. The photographer had never seen a priest in boots, so she took a picture of my feet next to the feet of the groom and best man. Imagine that in their wedding album! And the bride wanted her brother to be her witness, so we had to come up with a name for him other than **"Maid of Honor"** so we called him the **"Man of Honor"** for the day...... And I got to see some of my old parishioners one night. I put together a little gathering at a local restaurant figuring about 30 people might show up. Well, over 150 people showed up so we pushed the tables to the side and it felt like we were in a Vegas night club! And every time someone asked me if I were ever coming back to NJ, I told them **"NO!"**,but I would love to have them come out and visit me in Paradise!

Now I know why Pope John Paul II kissed the ground when he got off a plane....I was ready to do that when I touched down in Las Vegas late on Wednesday night. It is so awesome to be back here at home!

Back here at home, I found a box of stuff to unpack and I found a bargain I had bought a few years ago. I had been out rummaging in a second-hand store and I found an amazing bargain - a pair of tap shoes in my size. They were only $4, but were on sale for only $2. WOW! Now I can relive those great memories of my 3 years of tap dancing lessons when I was a kid! I'll bet most of you never knew I tap-danced as a kid! I'll also bet most of you never knew that I was one of the leads in the first school play ever at St. Joseph Regional High School when I was a student there. But my theatrical career was really short-lived. Two other leads failed a marking period grade and so were withdrawn from the play and it was never put on stage that year. But I'd like to tell you about the play anyway. It was written in 1955 and titled: **"The Billion Dollar Saint"** and it was about St. Francis of Assisi suddenly appearing on the campus of an upscale Jesuit university in the 1950's. This seems particularly appropriate this weekend since the feast day of St. Francis of Assisi is October 4th.

Needless to say, the presence of a bare-footed, brown-robed monk from the 1200's appearing and preaching poverty caused a bit of a stir on campus and among the higher-ups of the university. And he asked the most annoying questions! In the pivotal scene of the play, St. Francis is hauled into the office of the president ofthe university. The contrast is startling: St. Francis in his dingy brown robes and sandals; the president in a tailor-made dark business suit. And St. Francis says he wants to ask some questions about the educational process at the university. He begins with: **"Do the graduates who get Bachelor's Degrees love God?"** And the response is **"I suppose they do."** Then he continues with: **"Do those who get Master's Degrees love God**

more than those with Bachelor's Degrees?" And the response is **"Probably not, it has nothing to do with it."** And then St. Francis continues with: **"And do those who get PhD's love God more than those with Master's Degrees?"** And the exasperated president fairly screams, **"I don't know, it has nothing to do with it!"** To which St. Francis responds, **"Then why bother educating them if you're not teaching them to love God more and more?"**

I think St. Francis in the play is definitely on to something here. We start simply with our love of God and we need to keep nurturing it and expanding it as we grow in years and in the Catholic Faith. Today's First reading from Genesis starts us very simply with an insight into God's plan for the human race: **"The Lord God said: It is not good for the man to be alone. I will make a suitable partner for him."** And so the Bible begins the story of the human race continuing beyond Adam down to our own day.

To most of us this really seems elementary, even silly perhaps, but here we are witnessing the beginning of humanity, the pattern of the family, the procreation of children. Along with all the rest of creation, this too is good as God intended it. It is into this human setting that God would eventually send His only Son, Jesus Christ. It is into this human setting that each of us has been born and continues to live. In is within this human setting that along with God, we will work out our eternal salvation.

Today we celebrate **RESPECT LIFE SUNDAY.** Today we are reminded that human life is a special gift from God Himself, a very special gift that each of us shares, a special gift that makes possible everything else in life. All that affects the quality of that life or even its very existence is clearly a concern to us as Catholics and as human beings. Abortion which kills an innocent human being is not a right of women or men, it is a sin. Euthanasia (falsely termed "mercy-killing") is not mercy, but it surely is killing. The increasing dissolution of families, the breakdown of family life, the number of children in these situations - these are all areas of concern to us in our world today. We need to acknowledge them and work to solve them or at least minimize their effects and extent in our society.

If we are not growing in the love of God, then we are not doing something worthwhile with our lives. On this weekend of St. Francis, may we come to love and respect all life as a gift from God. May we be grateful for the gift of life for ourselves and for those around us among our families and friends. And may we prayerfully acknowledge our gratitude to God for allowing us to share in this life now so we can someday share in eternal life with God in heaven. As with most any other gift we ever receive, if we're really grateful for it, then we'll learn to use it well. We only get to go through this life once. We need to give it our best effort no matter what age we currently are.

By the way, in the play **"The Billion Dollar Saint"**, I didn't play St. Francis. I played the local Franciscan pastor who was told to **"Do something"** about this saint who was running around telling people that it is more important to learn to love God than to learn anything else. In real life, I hope I wouldn't have stopped him; I hope I would have joined him. **And I hope you would have joined him too.**

God bless you!

No comment is necessary. We look happy!

28th Sunday in Ordinary Time - "B"

11 October 2009

FIRST READING: Wisdom 7:7-11
PSALM: Psalm 90: 12-17
SECOND READING: Hebrews 4:12-13
GOSPEL: Mark 10:17-30

It is difficult to enter the Kingdom of God, but it is not impossible!

Hard to believe that Paradise could get any better, but when the weather cools off like this, it really is even more awesome here! One of the parishioners brought me back some great dried cherries from Michigan, and then had some lentil soup, chocolate cake, and even a homemade pizza, and a homemade pasta primavera with fresh mushrooms, peppers, zucchini and pasta shaped like little houses. I blessed over 45 animals last Sunday at our pet blessing in honor of St. Francis....mostly dogs, but a few cats and one turtle. Discovered that chihuaha's don't like holy water! And today we have our parish picnic from 1:00 PM to 4:00 PM at Spirit Mountain Park. Locals and visitors are welcome....just bring some food to share and join in the fun. And I loved all the **"Welcome Home"** greetings last weekend, and even the spike in the collection! I would have really been worried if it had spiked up only on the weekend I was away! I still think the slogan for Laughlin should be: **"Laughlin.... it just keeps getting better and better!"** Visitors come to us from all over the world. I'm glad people like to travel, and come see us here in Paradise!

Speaking of travel.....Today we take for granted that the world is round. In the 15th century, most people believed the world was flat. They thought monsters waited near the edge, and if you jour-neyed too far, you would fall right off the edge of the world. People laughed at or even jailed others who dared to think the world was round.

Since Columbus Day is on Monday, I thought I'd ask a few questions about Columbus. Not too many years ago, virtually every school child would know a little bit about this occasion, but now it seems to have fallen into the category of **"Days on which stores have big sales!"**

1. In what country was Christopher Columbus born?

   ITALY

2. For what country did Christopher Columbus sail?

   SPAIN

3. Name the King and Queen who supported the voyage?

   FERDINAND AND ISABELLA

4. In what year did his great discovery of the new world take place?

1492

5. How many ships did Columbus have in the expedition?

Three

6. Name them?

THE NINA, THE PINTA, THE SANTA MARIA

7. Where did Columbus think he had landed?

INDIA

8. What did he name the inhabitants?

INDIANS

9. Where was the first Columbus Day celebrated?

New York City

10. In which state was the first Columbus Day holiday?

COLORADO

Don't worry, there won't be a test on this next week, but I thought it was good for us all as a group to know a little bit of our American history. Nothing deep, just a little overview. Real study takes time and effort. Back in the days when I was teaching full time, I used to offer this little prayer at the beginning of every important test: **"May this test truly show the amount of time and effort you have put into your studies over the marking period. Amen."** And all the students would say **"AMEN!"** I know the prayer made some students very confident....for they had studied. And I know this prayer probably made some of the students very uncomfortable to realize that they had just prayed that the truth be shown as to how much study and effort they had actually done!

I thought of that little prayer several times this past week and I think it has some application in all of our lives. **"May this test truly show the amount of time and effort you have put into your studies over the years."**

In a way, life is really a competition, a test. It is something we actually do prepare for not only by our studies, but by our choices, our recreation, our sense of values, our faithfulness to God. And the results of all we have done in our lives eventually will be known completely when we meet God in eternity. But on a very practical level, those results are shown in how we face the current situations in our lives right now. How we deal with our families, how we concentrate on our studies, how we give an honest day's work for an honest day's pay, how we face problems and difficulties in our own lives and in the lives of those we love. These are all part of our efforts to learn and practice the elements of our Catholic Faith.

When people come to me for confession, I frequently tell them to confess their sins exactly as God sees them. You can't be more honest than that! God knows the time and effort and preparation we have put into living our lives, and only God can make valid judgments as to the goodness or sinfulness we display. If we confess our sins as God sees them, perhaps we too will learn to see them as God sees them, and maybe that will help us to make the efforts needed to correct them. As today's reading from the Letter to the Hebrews points out, God knows the thoughts of our hearts and it is to God that each of us must answer for our thoughts and actions. Of course, it also means that God knows the good we have accomplished even when no one else knows or notices or cares about it. And it is ultimately God's opinion that we should be concerned about, and not the opinions of anyone else no matter how important he or she might think himself/herself to be.

In today's Gospel, Jesus looks with love at the young man and invites him to follow Jesus completely. And the young man went away sad because his possessions lead him away from God. And Jesus takes this opportunity to remind His disciples that it is indeed difficult to follow Him, it is difficult to enter the Kingdom of God. It is not automatic. It is a gift offered to us, but then we have to do what is necessary to accept the gift.

Perhaps the most important and memorable line in today's Gospel is Jesus' comment to His disciples: **"For human beings, it is impossible, but not for God. All things are possible for God."** I suggest this is precisely the wisdom of which the Book of Wisdom speaks today in the First Reading when it tells us to pray for wisdom, to plead for wisdom from God, and to value this God-given wisdom very highly. It will guide us on the pathways of our lives to where God wants us to be.

Some of us are facing important decisions about our lives and our health and our jobs and our families. Today's readings speak to us in our search for wisdom to make the right choices. In the competition of life, may our lives truly bear witness to the amount of time and effort we have put into seeking and practicing the wisdom that God offers. It is not always easy, and it is not always pleasant to choose to do what is right and to avoid doing what is wrong. But is it always worthwhile, it is always worth the effort, and it is always possible, for just as Jesus told us: **"For human beings, it is impossible, but not for God. All things are possible for God."**

God bless you!

Andrew, Sam and I

29th Sunday in Ordinary Time - "B"

18 October 2009

FIRST READING: Isaiah 53:10-11
PSALM: Psalm 33:4-5, 18-19, 20, 22
SECOND READING: Hebrews 4:14-16
GOSPEL: Mark 10:35-45

We should always have confidence in God because God has already loved us first and united Himself with each one of us.

Now I know why parents go gray! Eddie, whom I affectionately call **"my illegitimate son"**, had his expensive GPS stolen from his **BMW** this week up in Vegas. I really felt bad for him until he admitted that he had left the **GPS** on the front seat of his **BMW** in a shopping center parking lot at night but **FORGOT** to lock the doors! In my compassion for him, I told him **"Why didn't you just put a sign on the window saying:ROB ME, I'M STUPID!"**

Also up in Vegas, I was showing my brother Michael (the Steelers' Fan), the Arizona Cardinals' Socks I was given. He told me I should burn them! You know, it's scary how much I've learned about football this past year. I even know the Steelers are playing the Cleveland Browns today, and I actually found out why the Cleveland team is called the BROWNS! I have learned more about football this year than I ever knew in my life!

Michael and I stayed up real late **(REAL LATE)** on Tuesday night and decided to **"run some lines"** to sharpen our acting skills. We went online and found a dialogue about a man praying to God, and God answering his prayer, so we decided to act it out. **Logically, of course, I chose to be God in the skit.** We were trying so hard to **"out act"** each other and laughing so hard, that we lost track of the time until we realized that it was 2:00 AM!

Ah, another week in Paradise! We had a beautiful parish picnic last Sunday with more great foods than I could ever hope to mention. Thanks to all who came....and to all who cooked! Really blew my diet there and with a couple of buffets thisweek, and then some great apple pie, blueberry cheesecake, pumpkin roll and Filipino buns. I blessed a house and was given a homegrown pomegranate. I never even knew anyone around here grew their own pomegranates! It's been a great week! Laughlin just keeps getting better and better! It's a magical place! **No wonder people love to come here!**

You all know how much I love magic. And I am not shy at all when it comes to wanting to be on stage, especially in a magic show. A few years ago I was in the audience watching a well-known illusionist, Jonathan Pendragon, and he asked for a male volunteer. I got my hand up in the air real fast! I got up on stage and he handed me a breadstick. I looked at it, and he said: **"You seem disappointed. Tell you what I'm going to do. You can keep the breadstick, OR you can have what's behind the curtain!"** Now it was obvious that the real trick was behind the curtain, so that's what I chose. And the curtain opens and there I am standing in front of a very authentic-looking French guillotine. I was a bit scared. Then he put the breadstick in the device, dropped the blade, and chopped the breadstick in half. He asked me to examine the device, and while I was doing that, he got behind me, shoved me down and put my head through the hole, and locked me in. **"In a few moments, you're going to have the illusion of this basket rushing towards your face,"** he said, as he placed a large basket under my head. Deep down, I knew that he couldn't get away with chopping someone's head off each night, so I hoped there was some trick. I realized I was holding on to the sides of the guillotine, and I didn't know how it worked, so I didn't want to mess anything up. He then moved the basket to one side, and joked, **"No problem, I'll chip it in!"** With that he shoved the breadstick in under my neck and pulled the cord, and the blade came rushing down....well, obviously it was an illusion. The breadstick got chopped in pieces, but I'm okay. I had no idea how it worked, but I'm glad it worked. I had visions of someone having to call the bishop and notify him that I was decapitated in a theater during a magic show. I sometimes wonder if the news would have made him sad.

My reason for telling that story is simple: If I could have enough confidence in a magician I didn't even know to let him playfully tamper with my neck in a guillotine, why do I have such difficulty having confidence in a God Who has never ceased to show His love and care for me?

Today's readings, with all their concentration on Jesus' suffering and death, are really calls to us to have confidence in our God. God has loved us so much that He willingly became one of us, willingly lived among us and taught us, and willingly died on the cross for us. So when today's Second Reading tells us to **"confidently approach His throne of grace"** we should do so confidently, knowing we will always find God's mercy and favor and help. Why do we sometimes fail to trust, to have confidence in a God, Who became one of us, and who constantly makes Himself available to us through His Body and Blood in the Holy Eucharist. Why do we not have enough confidence in God to make it a priority for ourselves and our children to be here for Mass? Many families, thank God, do that every week. But many others, even some in our religious education program do not. I'm sure if some coach said **"If you don't come for practice, you're not going to be ready to be on the team,"** we'd have enough confidence in his judgment to be at practice. So why don't we extend at least that same level of confidence to the God of the universe?

Today at Mass, take a few minutes and just ask God to give you enough confidence in Him to let Him into your life in a realistic way, today, and every day. There is nobody in whom you can more securely place your trust than in God Himself.

Jesus tells us that we all will have crosses to carry in life, but as with the other things in our lives, it's a lot better walking along with Jesus than just trying to go it alone. Two are always better than one, especially when God is One of the two and you're the other one.

God bless you!

A Night Out In Vegas!

30th Sunday in Ordinary Time - "B"

25 October 2009

FIRST READING: Jeremiah 31:7-9
PSALM: Psalm 126:1-6
SECOND READING: Hebrews 5:1-6
GOSPEL: Mark 10:46-52

None are so blind as those who refuse to see.

I was over at the Chef's Food Fest on Thursday night where all the casinos put on an awesome display and tasting of their best foods. I enjoyed sampling some beers and wines, some salmon cakes, shrimp scampi, mushroom ravioli, caramel apple tarts, chocolate-covered strawberries, strawberry cheesecake lollipops and so much more. The most interesting item of the evening for me was deep-fried sauerkraut balls. They were awesome with a little German mustard on them! I met a lot of our parishioners at the event and one commented, **"I'll bet all this food is going to show up in your sermon this weekend!"** Of course, she was right. If I ever write a book about being here in Laughlin, I think one of my title choices would be **"Eating My Way Through Paradise!"**

But Laughlin isn't all food, there's entertainment too. Got to see a great ventriloquist this week - Kevin Johnson. A really fun show. Ventriloquism is such an amazing art form! I wish I could do it. Just think of the possibilities for fun I could have when someone comes into church! I have a friend back East who is a ventriloquist and he drives me crazy whenever we eat together. He'll sit across a table from me and talk to me in different voices without moving his lips until I scream something like **"Open your mouth, you're driving me crazy!"**

We're starting to get a lot of our snowbirds back for the winter. So glad to see them again. And I hope we're making you feel welcome back here in Paradise. If there's anything I can do, please let me know. We love company! We're glad you're here! If it weren't for our snowbirds and visitors, Laughlin just wouldn't be as much fun as it is. Last week, one of our visitors shook my hand coming out of Mass at the Riverside and told me, **"Father, I love the stories you make up!"** You should have seen the look on his face when I told him, **"I don't make them up..... my life really is like that! Welcome to my world!"**

I was up in Vegas for a funeral on Friday night, and when Bishop Pepe greeted me, he hugged me. Back in NJ, the bishop wouldn't ever let me get that close to him after the accidents where I set him on fire and pushed him down a flight of stairs. I love being out here!

Okay, now I'm caught up with my news. Let's look at the Gospel news.....In today's Gospel, Jesus and His disciples encounter a blind man - Bartimaeus.

He kept calling out to Jesus, and Jesus calls him over and asks him point blank: **"What do you want me to do for you?"** And he replies immediately **"Master, I want to see."** And immediately he receives his sight, and Jesus commends the man's faith, telling him **"Your faith has saved you."**

Just think about that scene for a moment with me. It's very sparse. There's not a lot to it, but it is so powerful and clear.

Think of Jesus.....walking with a crowd of disciples and onlookers, yet able to hear the cries of one lone individual, a blind man by the side of the road. Doesn't that at least suggest to you that our prayers will be heard by Jesus no matter what else is going on in the world or in our little worlds? We should never doubt God's interest in us no matter how insignificant we might think ourselves to be. To God, each one of us is important and worthy of being heard. Now that's an attitude to remember whenever we pray. Never forget that God can always hear you when you call out to Him. God's mind is not cluttered and distracted like our minds sometimes are. Thank God for that!

Think of the disciples and the crowd.....they tried to shut the man up because he was bothering them. But he obviously wasn't bothering Jesus. Those disciples and the crowd had completely missed Jesus' mission and message. Sure they were following Jesus around, but they certainly weren't good examples or good advertisements for Jesus' message! We all know people like that.....people who hang with the right people and look like they're "religious", but who frequently miss the boat when it comes toactually acting in a Christian (Christlike) way. If someone acts like that to you, feel sorry for them. Don't hate them, but don't let them get in your way to God either.

Think of the blind man, Bartimaeus....he didn't give up even when the crowd told him to shut up. He knew he wanted Jesus to help him and he would not let anything or anyone stop him. Now that's an attitude we all need to bring with us to prayer whether here in church or back at our homes. We know we need Jesus. So we should not ever let anyone or anything block our way to Him. Do we display the direct faith of the blind man? Or do we let ourselves become so distracted that our path to Jesus is so cluttered and winding that we never allow ourselves to get close to Him.

We need to make sure that no one or no thing ever distracts us from keeping our attention fixed firmly on the Lord. **Jesus has something for us that no one else has.** Something so powerful that even a blind man could see it and want it.

And we should too.

God bless you!

Happy Birthday from Mike Rayburn!

All Saints Day

1 November 2009

FIRST READING: Revelation 7:2-4, 9-14
PSALM: Psalm 24:1-6
SECOND READING: 1 John 3:1-3
GOSPEL: Matthew 5:1-12

Today is our most hopeful day! Today we celebrate what we all hope to be some-day - Saints!

Another beautiful week in Paradise! Some great chocolate chip cookies and the Knights of Columbus took me out to a lunch buffet, and a friend in NJ shipped me a box of Italian pastries and homemade chocolate candy. And I found some really cool Halloween candy in the shape of body parts so I've been able to offer people a treat when they come to the office....**"Would you like a finger? Or a liver?Or how about a small spleen?"**Went to a house-warming party for MurraySawChuck, a magician/friend up in Vegas, on Sunday. It began at 6:00 PM and ended at sunrise! Trust me, I was home here in Laughlin **BEFORE** sunrise! But I sure packed a lot of fun into the party! It was great just hanging out with over 150 magicians and their families. Murray even bought a pinata for the kids to play with and hung it up in the front yard. He told them that they would get candy and prizes when they broke it. So the kids attacked the pinata with golf clubs and baseball bats while we adults ran for cover! Unfortunately, Murray has never had a pinata before so he didn't know that he was supposed to actually **FILL** the pinata with candy and prizes! Murray doesn't have any children. Michael, Eddie and I got to hang out one night and we were talking about the shows in Laughlin. Eddie's only 25 so when I was telling him about Mel Tillis being here, he said **"Who?"** So I tried to explain...**"You know, MMMMMelTillis!"** And he still didn't get it. Michael finally just looked across the table at me and said, **"Let it go, Charlie, let it go!"** I've got to stop hanging out with really young people!

Last weekend, one of our parishioners suggested that I come to Mass this weekend dressed as my favorite saint since it would be Halloween and All Saints Day. I smiled as I told him, **"But you don't know who my favorite saint is!"** He looked at me, and said, **"I'm bringing a camera!"** Actually I have several favorite saints so I thought I'd talk about saints today, and not get dressed up.

Back when I was teaching high school, I decided to get my sophomores all enthused about All Saints Day. I started talking about the great saints of the past and the lives they had led for the Lord. I was really going strong when I told them we should all want to be saints. And that someday after my time on earth, All Saints Day would be my feast day when I was enjoying heaven with God! All of a sudden, my class started smiling, and I was thrilled that I had reached them with my message. I should have just enjoyed the moment, but I had to foolishly ask them, **"Are you happy that someday I'm going to be a saint?"** They said, **"No, we're happy that someday you're going to be dead!"**

We celebrate All Saints Day today, a day on which we honor those men and women who have reached their final goal of spending eternity with God in heaven. Our first reading from the Book of Revelation describes the **"great multitude, which no one could count, from every nation, race, people, and tongue"** standing before God's throne and celebrating. And the Gospel speaks of our reward being great in heaven. So what can I tell you about saints today, those men and women who have reached their final goal?

Saints are sinners who kept on trying. They never gave up on themselves becoming the people God wanted them to be. There's a lesson in that for us. Don't give up. Of course, we're not as holy, or as good, or as kind, or as pure as we want to be. That's because we're not saints yet. But someday we will be as long as we keep on trying. If you remember nothing else that I say today, never forget that **"saints are sinners who kept on trying."** It's the most important thing I'm going to tell you.

Saints come in all shapes and sizes, males and females, married and single, young and old, educated and uneducated. Some are priests, some are little children, some lived long lives and died of old age, some had their lives cut short by martyrdom or illness. When I was in the seminary, we used to make up saints that seemed funny to us. We created **St. Rotunda**, a nun who ate so much that she got so big she couldn't leave her room so she became a hermit and thus became a saint. Or **St. Figita in Tormentis**, the patron saint of noisy and lively children. Or **St. Congola**, whom we imagined being killed for the Faith in Africa. We even made up a prayer to him: **"St. Congola, martyred in Africa, please take the spear out of your ear and hear my prayer."**

But the real saints did some amazing things in their lives. St. Simon Stylites wanted to get away from the world, so he built a pillar 30 feet high and lived on it for years. St. Jerome lived in a cave in Bethlehem and devoted his life to translating the Bible into Latin so it would be available to the people of the Roman Empire. He's credited with the famous line, **"Ignorance of the Scriptures is ignorance of Christ."** St. Francis of Assisi preached a love of God and nature that still resounds in our hearts and world today. St. Margaret Mary taught us the love of God through devotion to the Sacred Heart of Jesus. The Blessed Mother continues to teach us to follow her Divine Son faithfully. St. Therese of Liseaux who died at the age of 24 promised she would spend eternity doing good on the earth. St. Anthony helps us to find lost things.

There are saints for every time and place, saints for every profession. Most of us bear names of patron saints and hopefully share a saint's name with our children when we have them baptized. We are all called to become saints, to keep on trying until we get to heaven. We're not all the same. We don't all do the same things or become holy in the same ways. But we are all called to become the saints God wants us to be.

Never give up. And never forget what I told you a few minutes ago in this sermon:

"Saints are sinners who kept on trying!"

They did it, and so can we!

God bless you!

Two Great Guys and One Proud Priest!

32nd Sunday in Ordinary Time - "B"

8 November 2009

FIRST READING: 1 Kings 17:10-16
PSALM: Psalm 146:6-10
SECOND READING: Hebrews 9:24-28
GOSPEL: Mark 12:38-44

What do our lives say about us? Do our lives demonstrate that we are a people of faith, a people who believe in the love that God has for us?

I went to an awesome Halloween Party across the river last Saturday night. I went dressed as a priest....quite an effective costume since some of the guests didn't know I really am a priest! Life is good here in Paradise!

I met a man yesterday over at the hospital who was wearing two watches....one on each arm. I asked him why he had two watches on, and he told me one was Nevada time, and the other was Arizona time. I asked how he told them apart, and he told me it was easy - LEFT is for Laughlin. Actually I think he has a good idea! I might have to start doing that. It sure would help living here along the river.

The highlight of the week was when Michael and I went to San Francisco for two days. Got great cheap airfare (only $44), and found a hotel online near

Fisherman's Wharf for only $36 a night! The discount price should have tipped us off that there may be some small problems with it......After we booked it, we read some of the reviews. **Out of 248 ranked hotels in San Francisco, this one ranked 229 which means there are only 19 hotels in San Francisco ranked WORSE than it!** One of our friends thought it might be in a bad neighborhood and that Michael might get "hit on". Apparently there was no worry that someone might try to "hit on" me there! We both brought our own sheets and pillowcases....just in case! Actually, it wasn't too bad. There was a dead palm tree in front of our room, some holes in the sheets, a few light bulbs were missing, the fan wasn't fully attached to the ceiling, the closet door was hanging by one hinge, and you had to play with the toilet to flush it. And we're still not sure if those red stains we saw were blood or not. We stripped the beds before getting into them. But we had a lot of fun anyway, and some amazingsourdough bread and seafood and Italian food. We rode cable cars all over the place, and enjoyed all sorts of street entertainers throughout the city. We found an old penny arcade place (which now charged a quarter for each of the games) and we ended up playing each other in pinball and skeeball and a whole bunch of other early mechanical games. Michael got over 1,640,000 points in a pinball game.....I got about 300,000. I need more practice!

Even got a discount on my bus pass. The ticket booth salesman asked Michael how old I was. Michael told him I was 61. The guy said I looked older. So we ended up getting a senior citizen discount for me because I looked **OLDER** than 65! Darn! I've got to do something about that! It was fun to be in San Francisco, but it is great to get back here to Paradise!

A number of years ago, while having coffee after one of the Masses, I was sitting across from a parishioner who was drinking coffee and eating a cookie. After watching him for a few minutes, I asked him if he had just given up smoking. He looked at me with great surprise and said, **"Yes, but how did you know? I haven't told anyone yet."** I told him **"You're the only person I've ever seen who attempted to put out his cookie in an ash tray."**

My first pastor used to have a rule that a priest always had to be in the rectory. Of course, we had three priests so this was possible to do. But occasionally, when I was on duty, I would have to run out and I used to wonder how Father McGarry could always tell when I had just rushed in ahead of him. So one day, I deliberately hid in the garage and watched him park his car next to mine, and then immediately walk over to my car and put his hand on the hood and mutter to himself, **"It's still warm.... he's been out again!"**

I call these things **GIVEAWAYS**, actions that speak volumes about what is going on inside a person. Our San Francisco hotel's price was a **GIVEAWAY** about what we might find there. I could tell about the parishioner's smoking habits by his actions. Father McGarry could tell if I had been out by the warmth of my car engine. In today's Gospel, Jesus points out another **GIVEAWAY** to His disciples. As they stand by the collection box, Jesus calls their attention to a poor widow putting in two small coins worth only a few cents. **"This poor widow put in more than all the others for they donated from their surplus wealth, but she from her poverty has contributed all she had."**

Doubtless her two coins, literally her two cents' worth, was for Jesus a **GIVEAWAY** about her life-style and values. She gave all that she had. Like the widow in today's first reading, she gave what she had to God and trusted God enough to let Him do what He wants with it.

In an older translation, the coins were referred to as MITES, and so this Gospel came to be known as the Widow's M-I-T-E. An older commentator did a play on the word and said it really should be called the Widow's M-I-G-H-T because it shows the power and strength of her faith in God.

We might do well this week to spend some time looking to see what our **GIVEAWAYS** show about us. Do we really trust our friends and neighbors?

Do we really trust our parents and children? Do we really trust God? If so, how do we show this trust? If not, what can we do to develop the MIGHT of the widow in today's Gospel?

If people see the way we behave toward one another here at church, or at the store, or on the road, or in the casinos, or at school, they can see the **GIVEAWAYS** in our lives. Hopefully they will see us acting like people whose lives have been influenced by Jesus Christ. Otherwise, what they see might end up being a bad advertisement for the Catholic Faith we profess. So what will the **GIVEAWAYS** in your lives say about you this week? What would you like them to say?

God bless you!

33rd Sunday in Ordinary Time - "B"

15 November 2009

FIRST READING: Daniel 12:1-3
PSALM: Psalm 16:5, 8-11
SECOND READING: Hebrews 10:11-14, 18
GOSPEL: Mark 13:24-32

Lord, help me to remember that nothing is going to happen to me today that you and I together can't handle.

Life in Paradise is good, real good! I've been eating banana chocolate chip nut bread, lasagna rolls with spinach and cheese filling, caramel apple pie, macadamia nut candy, and even got some gift certificates for a few pounds of chocolate for later on in the year. Father Peter and I went out for our monthly lunch and he invited all of us over to see the new church building at St. Margaret Mary's in Bullhead City today from 1:30 PM to 5:00 PM (Arizona time). American, Mexican and Filipino foods and a fun afternoon, plus a tour of the beautiful new church they are building. I'm heading over after the Noon Mass. I've already seen the church building, but I don't want to miss out on the food! I hope a lot of our parishioners head over to see the progress on the new building. We're really happy for the spirit of cooperation between St. Margaret Mary and St. John the Baptist. On Veterans Day, I was the guest speaker at Desert Lawn Cemetery and even got quoted correctly in the local newspaper reminding people that there is always a price for freedom, and veterans know that price better than anyone else. And the American Heroes Museum reopened on Veterans Day over in Fort Mohave. It's worth checking out the history it preserves and displays. On a less serious note, I got up to Vegas to see a show called **FREAKS**, and felt right at home with my friends who do sword-swallowing, glass-eating, contortion, and other freaky things! A few years ago, they named me an honorary freak.....I'll have to tell you that story sometime. Spent part of my day off with Michael and Eddie in a COSTCO store in Vegas.....there were so many food samples being given out that we actually had our lunch there for free! I love being out here!

Eddie turns 26 next week and while we were talking, he asked **"Charlie, do you have a good will?"** I looked at him and said, **"Yeah, I'm pretty happy with it, but shouldn't you wait until I'm dead to ask the question?"** He just looked at me and explained that he meant did I have a GOOD WILL store in the Laughlin area so he could give me some clothing to donate. But his question was just one of a few I've been asked recently so I thought I would tell you about them.

In the past couple of weeks, I have been asked to give advice on a number of issues. A young friend of mine, in his late 20's, was bemoaning the fact that his girlfriend had dropped him and he couldn't figure out why. So he emails me saying that he just can't understand women. Then he adds: **"You're old....does it ever get any easier to figure things out?"**

Another friend questioned me about suffering and death, and why do I believe in God when even good people suffer and evil people seem to get away with things and prosper.

Since these are questions that might be on the mind of several people, I thought I'd answer them briefly today.

As far as suffering and death go, they are part of life. We can't escape them. And even being **"good"** doesn't take them away. The Bible does not teach us that God will remove suffering and death from those who are faithful. But the Bible does tell us something very important about them. In today's Gospel, for example, Jesus talks about the end of the world, and terrible calamities like the sun and moon being darkened and the stars falling from the sky. But Jesus ends his speech by telling His disciples **"Heaven and earth will pass away, but My words will not pass away."** All along, Jesus has been telling His disciples as He tells us today that He will not leave us, He will not abandon us, He will always be with us. Today, Jesus reminds us that, yes, tragedies and problems of all sorts will come. They may be personal or they may be cosmic - my own little world might come crashing in on me because of some personal tragedy or bad news, or the whole world might come to an end in my lifetime. BUT (and it is a BIG BUT!) no matter what happens, Jesus has made a promise to us that He will be with us through it all. We all know tragedies and problems will come, but we sometimes need to be reminded that with God we can face any and all of them.

And my young friend's question to me: **"You're old...does it ever get any easier to figure things out?"** I thought about that one for a long time. My immediate reaction is: **"Kid, it doesn't get any easier no matter how old you get or how old you think I am!"** There will always be things we just don't understand in life. But as I thought about it a little more, my reaction became more level-headed. If I really believe that God is with me, then maybe I don't need to figure things out as much as I need to trust that God knows more than I do. Maybe that's the benefit of getting older in the Faith, realizing that God knows what He's doing even when He doesn't explain it to me.

My prayer today is one that we might all share in **"Lord, help me to remember that nothing is going to happen to me today that You and I together can't handle."**

That's a truth to remember: **"Lord, help me to remember that nothing is going to happen to me today that You and I together can't handle."**

God bless you!

Family Time for My Birthday!

Solemnity of Our Lord Jesus Christ the King

22 November 2009

FIRST READING: Daniel 7:13-14
PSALM: Psalm 93:1-2, 5
SECOND READING: Revelation 1:5-8
GOSPEL: John 18:33-37

I never noticed that before! There are signs all around us, every day that we live.

I love making lists. So you may have noticed that each week I make a list of all the things that make life here in Paradise so awesome. This week my list includes chocolate chip cookies and peanut butter cookies, donuts, and sharp cheddar cheese from Wisconsin. It includes having the church floor completely cleaned so that it looks almost brand new. It includes shipping out another 100 or so boxes for our troops thanks to your generosity. It includes a fun birthday party for two of our parishioners on Thursday night.

My list also includes seeing Frank Marino's **DIVAS LAS VEGAS** at the Riverside a few times this week. Now before you start wondering, the reason I'm seeing the show a few times is not because I'm thinking of becoming a female impersonator, but because it's a really funny show, and because my friend Paul is the dance captain. If you see the show, he's easy to pick out.....just look at the male dancers and try to guess which one is least likely to know me, and that should point you to Paul! And Frank Marino's Joan Rivers is incredible! I saw the show some years ago in Vegas with my Mom when she was in her 80's, and I wondered how she would react to seeing female impersonators on stage. After the show, I asked her about the show, and all she said was **"Those women have such beautiful gowns!"** It's worth a look, and it will give you more than a few smiles.

My list also includes celebrating Eddie's 26th birthday up in Vegas. We gave Eddie a choice of picking a night to go out to celebrate, or just getting hit 26 times with a baseball bat. He wisely chose to go out. So Michael and I took him to see Lance Burton's show at the Monte Carlo on Tuesday night, and then we said we'd take him out to a **tapas** bar we had found. **Tapas** are interesting snacks or small appetizers, and the idea is to order a whole bunch of different ones and share them. So we get to the place, order a pitcher of red sangria, and a bunch of tapas from the menu. We're having a great time, but notice that Eddie is looking around as if he's trying to see something. So we asked him, **"What are you looking for?"** And he tells us that we told him we were bringing him to a **TOPLESS** bar and he hasn't seen anyone topless yet! "Eddie, it's a **TAPAS** bar, not a **TOPLESS** bar! Do you really think we would be bringing you to a **TOPLESS** bar?" Now that's a story we'll be telling for years to come! He and Michael both got carded when we sat down to play some roulette. **I never get carded!** I never even got carded when I was under 21! And, yes, they did have cameras back then in the age of the dinosaurs!

But like I said, I really love lists, and recently learned something about an ancient list...the Seven Wonders of the Ancient World. What I learned is that the list was originally put together not for historical purposes but for tourism! These were the places that an ancient Greek traveler should want to see!

Can you name the **SEVEN WONDERS OF THE ANCIENT WORLD**? The only one I knew right away was the **GREAT PYRAMID IN EGYPT** because it's still standing and I have actually been to see it. The others I had to look up. **THE HANGING GARDENS OF BABYLON, THE TEMPLE OF ARTEMIS AT EPHESUS,THE STATUE OF ZEUS AT OLYMPUS, THE MAUSOLEUM OF MAUSSOLIOS AT HALICARNASSUS, THE COLOSSUS OF RHODES** and **THE LIGHTHOUSE AT ALEXANDRIA** - all of which have been destroyed.

This reminded me of a wonderful story of a teacher who was teaching ancient history in a grammar school. And she asked her young students to name the seven wonders of the world, and then to share their lists. Of course, many of the students had no idea of the ancient world, so they listed things like the Empire State Building, the World Trade Center Towers, Yellowstone National Park, the Grand Canyon, St. Peter's Basilica, and the TajMahal.

But one little girl in class had remained silent. When the teacher comes up to her, she says **"I don't think I understood the assignment. I don't have any of those answers."** So the teacher encourages the girl to share her list, and she says: **I THINK THE SEVEN WONDERS OF THE WORLD ARE: To see...to hear...to touch...to smell...to feel...to love...and to laugh.**

Sometimes on our journey through life we miss the wonder of the ordinary. The real wonders of the world are given to us by God. And sometimes we can be so busy looking for man-made or larger-than-life wonders that we miss the ones we already have right now with us and within us. We miss seeing the story of our lives and the signs God gives to each one of us.

Today's feast of **CHRIST THE KING** is a powerful concept. Jesus really is **KING**, but He rules a kingdom that is different from what this world expects. He has no armies, and no palaces. He rules in the hearts and lives of people who follow Him. He has already shared His wonders with us but we sometimes take them for granted and think of them as too common to be important, when in fact they are awesome gifts to us from a King beyond this world's imagination! All we have to do is notice them, see them as signs of God's love for us, and His care in directing us throughout our lives.

As we honor Jesus Christ today as **KING** of the universe, we need to honor the generous gifts He has given to us. It is a wonder, a miracle in fact, that we can **SEE, HEAR, TOUCH, SMELL, FEEL, LOVE** and **LAUGH.** And it is through these seemingly ordinary gifts that Jesus' Kingdom will be spread.

For many of us, I think, the truly spiritual life of Christ the King within each one of us begins with a simple sentence: **"I never noticed that before."** So much happens in life that so many fail to notice. And they miss all the signs around them. We can and should do so much better than that! Even a sort-of-old guy like me can learn to do it. And so can you, no matter if you're young or old. This week, honor Christ as King by noticing and honoring the astounding gifts He has already given to us, and by using them well and appreciating them. Take the time to really **SEE, HEAR, TOUCH, SMELL, FEEL, LOVE** and **LAUGH** a lot. And you will see so very much that you never noticed before. It can change your lives. And Christ's Kingdom will grow.

God bless you!

Charlie, Charlie, Paul!

First Sunday of Advent - "C"

29 November 2009

FIRST READING: Jeremiah 33:14-16
PSALM: Psalm 25:4-5, 8-9, 10, 14
SECOND READING: 1 Thessalonians 3:12-4:2
GOSPEL: Luke 21:25-28, 34-36

***We are waiting for Christmas once again,
and we know for Whom we are waiting!***

Thanksgiving Week in Paradise has been awesome! A delicious turkey dinner with some incredible baked squash with butter and brown sugar, a couple of turkey sandwiches with friends, some homemade Polish pirogi's, and cute little turkeys made from Oreo's and candy corn. Last weekend, I was able to go out for a late Sunday breakfast with some friends in the show **DIVAS LAS VEGAS**. They had show comps for the buffet here at the Riverside, so when we got there with the comps the cashiers at the buffet knew we were all from the show. And they were curious which parts we played. My friend Paul told them he was a dancer, Mitch said he worked as a special assistant to the star of the show, and before I could think of something, Paul told them that I was in the show playing **BEYONCE**! Bet that left those cashiers wondering a lot! I think I'll keep my day job! As I told the nearly 140 people at Mass on Thanksgiving Day, we all have a lot for which to be thankful here in Paradise. If we live here, or if we get to visit here for a few days or months each year, this is a very special place. If you haven't done so already, take some time to look around and be thankful for where we are. We are a very fortunate people, we should be a very grateful people.

Like so many others, I went out shopping on Black Friday. It wasn't as bad as I thought it would be, and I got some great deals! But I really don't like waiting in line. I see too much! I was waiting in line recently at a local drug store and the person in front of me had hauled 8 packages of tissues up to the checkout counter. The clerk explained to her that they were not the brand on sale, so they would be the regular price. **OH NO!** She wanted to sale price! Well, the clerk volunteered to go and get her 8 packages of the tissues that were on sale. Well, that just wouldn't do! She wanted **THESE** 8 boxes of tissues, but at the sale price! I thought my head would explode!

Then I was in the food store, and the woman in front of me in line wanted to return a container of sour cream that she bought **TWO WEEKS AGO** because it now had an expired date on it! I did not mentally handle that well.

But the clincher was at the post office (fortunately not the one in Laughlin!) as a customer counted out pennies to pay for mailing a package. Oh, the pennies weren't in a change purse or plastic bag, or anything as simple as that! They were scattered all over her pocketbookl. Then, when I finally got to the counter, the clerk told me that he didn't have time to weigh my handful of letters because it would take too long! I should have sorted them by weight and country before I came to the post office!

Waiting is not something I do well. Delays usually upset me. Back in New Jersey, I used to hate being in a toll booth line for exact change when the person in the car in front of me has no clue where he has the exact change as he fumbles around the car.

I guess none of us really likes waiting. But waiting is what this season of Advent is all about. Over the next four weeks, we will be given the opportunity to **WAIT FOR CHRISTMAS**. We might spend a lot of time waiting for lines to move in traffic and at checkout counters, waiting for store clerks to help us, waiting for family members and friends to gather, even waiting for Santa to come. Ultimately, it is all **WAITING FOR CHRISTMAS.**

And we're in good company! The Israelites waited for Jesus to come for thousands of years. Mary waited expectantly for the nine months that she carried Jesus in her womb. And today, as Advent begins, we join in waiting for Jesus Christ all over again.

Sure, there's a lot to be done between now and Christmas, but don't lose sight of the beauty of waiting. In a world filled with broken dreams and empty promises, in a world that seems so very insecure, in a world where hope seems so fragile, there's something very beautiful, very comforting, about waiting for Christmas, and knowing that God still keeps His promises. Knowing that since the beginning of time itself, God Himself has waited for each one of us. God certainly knows how to wait, and we can learn.

As today's First Reading from the Prophet Jeremiah puts it: **"The days are coming, says the Lord, when I will fulfill the promise I made to the house of Israel and Judah."** And the Gospel reminds us that we need to be vigilant at all times during our waiting.

The more we wait for something, the more we eagerly expect it, the more we will appreciate it when it comes. As you write your Christmas cards, as you shop for your Christmas gifts, as you decorate your homes and listen to the Christmas music, try to see all of this as a set of reminders - the entire world is caught up in waiting for Christmas.

This Advent Season, every time you're kept waiting for someone or something, let it be a reminder to you that we're all waiting for Jesus, waiting to celebrate once again God's faithfulness to us.

We know beyond any doubt **WHO** we are waiting for. When you say **"Merry Christmas"** over the next few weeks, you're reminding everyone around you that you really do know **WHO** you are waiting for! Jesus Christ really is the only reason for this season.

God bless you!

"Oh, if I only had hair like Murray!"

Second Sunday of Advent - "C"

6 December 2009

FIRST READING: Baruch 5: 1-9
PSALM: Psalm 126: 1-2, 2-3, 4-5, 6
SECOND READING: Philippians 1:4-6, 8-11
GOSPEL: Luke 3:1-6

These are not just imaginative stories, these are accounts of what really happened in real places at real times to real people.

Well, at least we're not getting any snow in Paradise like some other parts of our great country this weekend. Just one more thing for which to be thankful here...in addition to the bacon cheese quiche, deviled eggs and other goodies that came my way this week. Our Thanksgiving collection amounted to $818 for the Colorado River Food Bank so we're grateful that we can share the good things God has given to us. I've been accumulating a lot of pictures and things on my computer so I went out to buy an external hard drive. Got a great buy...only $49....now I have over 500 gigs of memory. Have no idea how much that really is, but it sure sounds like a lot. I'm not even sure I've ever remembered that much stuff in my life. But the highlight of my week was getting to meet Eddie Ifft. Now I'm guessing most of you don't know who he is, but he's a young comedian out of Pittsburgh,

PA. (see I know something else about Pittsburgh besides the Steelers!) I saw him on YouTube about 5 years ago, and bought one of his CD's figuring I may be able to use some of his material. Well, I got it home and put it into my CD player and cranked up the volume so my secretary could hear it too. Unfortunately, he came out with a string of really bad words so I had to shut it down right away. Later in the day, I got to listen to it privately and was really bothered by it. He was really talented and had some great comic story lines, but he messed them up with the language. So I emailed him........ And I told him if he ever performs near where I live, I'll be there in the first row to make him nervous. He was at the Improv in Vegas this week, so I got to see his act and met up with him after the show. I congratulated him and said, **"I'm Charlie"** and he pointed to his collar and said **"This Charlie?"** We got to hang out between shows on Tuesday night. We remembered our past conversations and had a great time catching up with each other. I tried to memorize some of his act, and may be using it later on in the year. He's really cleaned up his language and is really funny.

There is something powerful about memorizing something, and knowing it exactly word-for-word. In my past, I had many teachers who insisted on having us memorize things. One person who stands out in my mind is **Sister Flavian**. She was my 6th grade teacher. **Sister Flavian made us memorize our textbooks!** Each week, we had a different part of the book to memorize. One week I had to memorize the entire climate of Europe (about 6 paragraphs!). There are still some places in Europe I won't ever visit because I know I wouldn't like the climate there!

I mention this little bit of my past for several reasons. **First**, to remind parents how very important it is for your children to learn some of their prayers by memory. A child old enough to receive First Holy Communion should be able to at least pray the Our Father and the Hail Mary without any difficulty. Prayers need to be said and reinforced in the home. **Second**, today is the annual SECOND COLLECTION for the Retired Religious priests, brothers and sisters in the United States. I ask you to be generous in this second collection to assist the religious men and women who, like Sister Flavian, were in a large part responsible for some if not all of our formation in the Catholic Faith.   And **third**, because I want to suggest that we try to memorize today's Gospel, or at least the first two verses of it:

> *In the fifteenth year of the reign of Tiberius Caesar, when Pontius Pilate was governor of Judea, and Herod was tetrarch of Galilee, and his brother Philip was tetrarch of the region of Idumea and Trachonitis, and Lysanias was tetrarch of Abilene, during the high priesthood of Annas and Caiaphas, the word of God came to John the son of Zechariah in the desert.*

Why memorize these two verses? I'm sure some of the kids are asking that, and some of you adults too. Because with these two verses we have an historical setting. There really was a **Tiberias Caesar** who ruled; there really was a **Pontius Pilate** who was governor of Judea; there really was a **Herod** who was ruler in Galilee....and **Philip** and **Lysanias** and **Annas** and **Caiaphas** were real people too. People who lived in a real time and place on this planet earth. **It was to real people, in our real world, at a real time in history, that the Word of God came.** The Gospel isn't some fairy tale or myth that takes place in a galaxy long, long ago and far, far away in someone's imagination. Jesus really came into our world and Jesus is really God. So God really came and lived among us.

If we could only realize this truth, we might for even a brief instant be able to comprehend how much God loves us and cares for us. And perhaps in that brief moment of real insight, we might decide to listen to the message that God came to teach us. Christmas celebrates a wonderful reality about God and His people. If we could only comprehend this a little, we would really have something big to celebrate this Christmas. Think about the reality that Christmas celebrates as we continue to get ready for it in the coming weeks. Christmas celebrates something that really happened. That's what makes it so very important.

God bless you!

One of us is in shape! And it's not me!

Third Sunday of Advent - "C"

13 December 2009

FIRST READING: Zephaniah 3:14-18
PSALM: Isaiah 12: 2-3, 4, 5-6
SECOND READING: Philippians 4:4-7
GOSPEL: Luke 3:10-18

John knew that there was One coming after him Who was mightier than anyone else in the world.

Okay, enough of this cold weather! This is Paradise! It's not supposed to be this cold! I was up in Vegas on Tuesday night to go out for dinner with a friend from NJ who was the local undertaker in my parish. He and I used to go out for lunch or dinner when I lived there. It was always fun when one of my parishioners would see us together in a restaurant. As soon as they came over to the table, I'd always say to them, **"Wow, so good to see you, we were just talking about you!"** Had a super time at our parish Christmas party on Friday night.....just under 400 people came for a great show and dinner and all-around great time. I got set of **homemade STEELERS' CHRISTMAS STOCKINGS** as an early Christmas present, but apparently my feet are not helping the STEELERS much this season. They've gone downhill so fast! In fact, my reputation has become so bad that I actually had an avid GREEN BAY PACKERS' fan come up to me and tell me **NOT** to wear the

Packers' socks because I would bring them bad luck! And the food highlight of my week was an amazing **APPLE FRITTER** that one of our Knights of Columbus brought back to me from a store in Lake Havasu. It was **THIS BIG**! And loaded with sugary glaze and pieces of apple. And it weighed a ton! I have to admit I didn't share it with anyone! Oh, and I got to see a friend up in Vegas that I had not seen in a few months. His first comment to me when he saw my hair was: **"What did you do? Stick your finger in a light socket?"** Hey, I'm liking my hair like this. **What it lacks in color, it is making up in height!**

Nine young soldiers had received overnight passes from their Army camp. When morning came, not one of the nine was present. An hour after their absence was noted, the first soldier straggled back into camp. He was immediately taken before his company commander. **"I'm sorry to be late, sir,"** the young soldier said, **"but I had a date, lost track of time, and missed the last bus. I wanted to make it back on time, so I took a taxi. Almost halfway back to camp, the cab broke down, so I went to the nearest farm and bought a horse. As I was riding on the horse, the animal suddenly fell to the ground and died. So I did the last miles on foot and here I am."** Although he was skeptical about the chain of weird excuses, the company commander let the young man off with a mild lecture on being punctual. Soon after, seven more stragglers reported in, one by one, each with the very same story! They had a date, lost track of time, missed the last bus, took a cab, cab broke down, bought a horse, horse fell dead. Finally, the ninth and last soldier arrived. Now totally exasperated, the company commander growled: **"What happened to you?"**The ninth man replied, **"Sir, I had a date, lost track of the time, missed the last bus, took a cab...."** "Wait a minute! Wait a minute!, " cried the company commander, **"Are you going to tell me that the cab broke down?"** "No, sir, " the soldier replied, **"the cab was fine. The problem was that there were so many dead horses blocking the road that we couldn't get through."**

I'm always amazed at the excuses people come up with for why they don't come to church, or why they don't follow the moral teachings they know are right. Sometimes we just get caught up in the busy-ness of life that we just make lame excuses for why we don't pay enough attention to the important stuff. It's the little things that get in the way sometimes. Little things that interrupt us.

Life is full of interruptions. People drop in unexpectedly **(It is as if they know the exact moment when we close the bathroom door!)**, phones ring at awkward times **(like the ever-present cell phones that ring in the middle of the school play or the consecration of the Mass),** unforeseen emergencies call us away from home in the middle of the At one time or another, this has happened to all of us - we have all been interrupted. And if we have developed great expectations about finishing whatever we do, life is going to cause us some painful frustration. Sometimes we don't even get a chance to finish a sentence before someone interrupts us.

John the Baptist, who is the central figure in today's Gospel, learned very early in his life what many of us will only discover after many years: namely that some of the things we hope for and work for the hardest will never be fully realized in our lifetime. We know it is so satisfying to actually finish a project or a task, and it is so hard to let it go unfinished and allow someone else to complete it.

Even John the Baptist must have found it hard to realize that his work would be unfinished in his lifetime, that he was only getting things ready for Someone Else...."**One mightier than I is coming.**"

As we prepare for the coming of Christ at Christmas, we should realize that our whole life (and not just these few days) should be a preparation for Christ to come into the world. But in many ways, we are working on a project that might not be completed in our lifetimes. We might not finish everything we had planned before we are interrupted by sickness or death or any one of the hundreds of other interruptions in our human lives. But maybe, just maybe, we did get things ready for the Lord just a little. And maybe, just maybe, that was just what the Lord wanted us to do.

John the Baptist tried to get the world ready for Jesus. All the great saints tried to get their world ready for Jesus. You and I have just less than two weeks left to try to get our hearts and homes and families and lives ready for Jesus. Oh, we may not finish everything, but please God let it be truly said of each one of us - we tried. **At the end of our lives, God is not going to ask us if we have succeeded completely. God is only going to ask us if we tried.**

So write those cards, buy those gifts, cook those meals, call those friends, wrap those packages.... but just remember that we're doing all this for the Lord. We're trying to get the world, our little part of it anyway, ready for the Lord to enter our hearts and the hearts of those around us. And all God asks of us is that we try. And there is no good excuse for not trying. None at all.

God bless you!

Adam is the Tall One! Christian and
I are the Other Ones!

Fourth Sunday of Advent - "C"

20 December 2009

FIRST READING: Micah 5:1-4
PSALM: Psalm 80: 2-3, 15-16, 18-19
SECOND READING: Hebrews 10:5-10
GOSPEL: Luke 1:39-45

Filled with the Holy Spirit, Elizabeth recognizes the presence of the Lord in the womb of the Blessed Virgin Mary.

Just heard about the snowstorm hitting the East Coast.....New Jersey is getting about a foot of snow this weekend. I sure don't miss worrying about plowing out the church parking lot! **Ah, it's good to be in Paradise!** Got treated to a fantastic brunch last Sunday here in Laughlin....tons of seafood.... crab, shrimp, lobster. They sure didn't make any money on me! And up in Vegas this week, a buddy of mine got comp tickets to see **CHER** so we enjoyed her show and all the great memories of **SONNY AND CHER** from the past. She's older than I am, and she still can move! Stayed up really late on Thursday night for a magical experience called **WONDERGROUND** featuring some of the best magical talents in Vegas. And you know I enjoyed that! It was at a HOOKAH Lounge and I kept hoping that it was only tobacco they were smoking! Toured the huge drive-through display of Christmas lights in Sunset Park.And enjoyed the huge Nativity display at the end. It just isn't Christmas without Christ and even this secular light display acknowledged that. That made me feel good.

I started writing my Christmas cards on Friday night. I know that some people write cards starting with **FAMILY**, and others do it **ALPHABETICALLY**, but I have my own system. I write my cards **GEOGRAPH-ICALLY**! I have written my foreign cards for Australia and France and England. This weekend I will write my East Coast ones, and hopefully work my way across the country in time for Christmas. If you don't get a card from me, it just means you live too close!

I was getting my hair cut this week (and getting that beautiful feeling of sheer pleasure as the stylist shampooed my hair and massaged my temples! Ah, they don't do that in NJ!). We got to talking about some coming events and she said we'd have to talk about that **"after we get past the birth-day"**. So I'm sitting there thinking what birthday she's talking about. My birthday isn't coming up for another month, her birthday is in the summer. **So whose birthday is she talking about?** You can only imagine how foolish I felt when I asked her whose birthday she was talking about. And she looked at me, with sharp scissors in her hand, and said **"JESUS' BIRTHDAY!"** Of all things for me to forget, how could I forget that Christmas is Jesus' birthday! Glad I have a hair stylist to write my sermons for me!

This Friday is Christmas! And Christmas is Jesus' birthday! **Don't be like me and forget that!** And today's Gospel for the 4th Sunday of Advent speaks of Mary. She is one of the central figures in the whole Christmas tradition. It was a human being, Mary of Nazareth, who first brought God to man. She was the instrument, the gateway, that God used to come into the history of the world as a man in the person of Jesus Christ.

Through all the intervening years, God has continued to travel the same route. He comes to men and women through other men and women. Through the **words**, the **warmth**, the **goodness**, the **kindness** of one person, God enters into the life of another person. This Christmas, bring God to others because you have learned there is no real life without God. Be an opportunity for Jesus to touch people's lives in your family, in your business, in your school, in your neighborhood. If you don't do that, who will?

Mary going to Elizabeth in today's Gospel is a model for all of us of the outreach that our Catholic Faith should inspire in us. **We have Something - rather, we have SOMEONE - Whom the world really needs!** There are countless people alive in the world today to whom God will come only through you. For these people, you can be as Mary was - a gate through which God can enter their lives.

And Christmas is the time to open that gate for all your family and friends.

God bless you!

Tommy Wind comes to Vegas!

Christmas (Mass at Midnight)

25 December 2009

FIRST READING: Isaiah 9:1-6
PSALM: Psalm 96:1-2, 2-3, 11-12, 13
SECOND READING: Titus 2:11-14
GOSPEL: Luke 2:1-14

Jesus Christ is born into our world to restore to us the hope of eternal life and happiness with Him.

I had a bad cold earlier this week, and I just started to shake it yesterday. I was talking with my brother Michael in Florida on the phone and told him about the congested sinuses, and the red drippy nose, and the deep voice when I tried to talk. I said I was worried it would last through the Christmas Masses. He told me I should be happy with the red nose..... it would remind the people of Rudolph the Red-Nosed Reindeer (and he reminded me **"You like to be in charge anyway, so who's more in charge than Rudolph leading Santa around!"**) And then he told me a lot of women like a deep sexy male voice. I told him that I was not looking to cultivate the image of a sexy male red-nosed reindeer for my Christmas sermon.

Mayor Oscar Goodman up in Las Vegas always says that he's the **HAPPIEST MAYOR IN THE WHOLE USA!** I want you to know that I'm the **HAPPIEST PRIEST IN**

THE WHOLE USA! I live in Paradise, and I get to go to Vegas every week. I have the newest parish in the Diocese of Las Vegas since we were designated as a parish last June, and I have the best parish in the whole diocese. My friends in show-biz complain that they can't find enough work, and I tell them that I've got a gig in Don's Celebrity Theatre three times every weekend with an open-ended contract.

Well, even here in Paradise (otherwise known as Laughlin) we have to be "politically correct", so let me wish you a **"Happy, Merry CHRISTMAHA-NUKAWANZA."** I think it's kind of interesting that virtually every store in the USA has been promising delivery of gifts by December 25th, but trying O, SO HARD to not admit that that date is significant! At least for today, let's scrap all that politically correct JUNK and admit what we all know is true: It's**CHRISTMAS**, not the winter solstice or "the holidays"; It's a **CHRISTMAS** tree, not a Hanukkah bush or a Holiday tree; and those are **CHRISTMAS** carols we're singing, not just some holiday songs. We gather to celebrate the most significant event since the creation of the world.....God Himself was born to live among us because He loves us! It's Christmas! Admit it!

I love Christmas! I love the lights, I love the decorations, I love the Christmas carols, I love the nativity sets, I love writing and reading Christmas cards, I love the cookies and other foods that are so plentiful at Christmas, and, yes, I really do love FRUITCAKE!

And I love the presents. I love giving presents and I love receiving presents. I love shaking the presents and trying to guess what each one contains. And no matter what gifts I end up receiving from my family and my friends, I am always thankful not only for the gift, but even more so for what the gift represents. A gift from a friend is a real treasure, no matter what the gift itself might be.

And speaking of friends.....A friend of mine sent me a Christmas email based on a famous Scripture passage from 1 Corinthians 13. The original passage is read frequently at weddings, but my friend shared a Christmas version of it with me as a gift and I'd like to share his gift with you:

If I decorate my house perfectly with plaid bows, strands of twinkling lights and shiny.If I slave away in the kitchen, baking dozens of Christmas cookies, preparing gourmet meals and arranging a beautifully adorned table at mealtime, but do not show love to my family and friends, I'm just another cook.

If I work at the soup kitchen, sing carols in the nursing home, and give all that I have to charity, but do not show love to my family and friends, it profits me nothing.

If I trim the tree with shimmering angels and crocheted snowflakes, attend a myriad of Christmas parties and sing with the choir, but do not focus on Christ, I have missed the point.

Love stops the cooking to hug the child.

Love sets aside the decorating to kiss the husband or wife.

Love is kind, though sometimes harried and tired.

Love remembers the people who are not alive with us this Christmas but who made Christmas so amazingly beautiful for us in the past.....grandparents, parents, spouses, children, life-long friends who have died. While they spend Christmas with the Lord, we do not forget them here.

Love doesn't envy another's home that has coordinated Christmas china and table linens.

Love doesn't yell at the kids to get out of the way. Love is thankful that they are there to be in the way.

Love doesn't give only to those who are able to give in return, but rejoices in giving to those who can't.

Love bears all things, believes all things, hopes all things, endures all things.

Love never fails.

Video games will break, pearl necklaces will be lost, golf clubs will rust. But giving the gift of love will endure forever.

Christmas celebrates the best gift of all - Jesus - Who came to share God's love with us. May we always be thankful for Jesus coming into our world and teaching us how to live and how to love. Jesus is the best gift of all. May we celebrate this Christmas by being thankful for all we have, and by sharing God's love for all the people who make up our lives.

Merry Christmas from all of us here at St. John the Baptist Catholic Church in Laughlin to all of you from near or far.

God bless you!

It must be Christmas!

The Holy Family of Jesus, Mary and Joseph

27 December 2009

FIRST READING:Sirach 3:2-6, 12-14
PSALM: Psalm 128:1-5
SECOND READING: Colossians 3:12-21
GOSPEL: Luke 2:41-52

Family is sometimes what we are born into as a gift from God. Family is sometimes something we create using the gifts God gives us.

Well, it's been a really busy week here in Paradise! Since Thursday (Christmas Eve), I've offered 13 Masses so I'm feeling mighty holy!

I'm guessing that our little saying **"See you in church!"** is really ringing true! It's been great seeing so many of you so many times in the past few days! I don't open my Christmas cards until I've finished writing mine, so some of my Christmas cards will really be Happy New Year cards by the time I'm done. Our Christmas Masses were so beautiful and so beautifully attended. It was great to get to meet so many of our visitors and to meet so many of the extended families of our local parishioners. I figure I should share some **"family"** information about me for those who don't know it already. I'm one of those **"only child"** persons. I always say that when my parents had me, they were so thrilled they didn't want anyone else. Some of my friends say that after my parents had me, they were too scared to have anyone else. My Dad died in his 50's when I was a teenager, and my Mom died 3 years ago in her 90's. So I've lived longer than my Dad already, and I'm hoping to beat my Mom too. My friend Michael and I are like brothers so we just go along with it and tell folks that we are brothers..... which is kind of fun since my background is **Lithu-anian** and Michael's is **Jamaican/Puerto Rican**. Somewhere along the way, we picked up Eddie, and he is the son I never had so he became my **"ille-gitimate son"**. And the three of us make up one of the most caring but strangely weird families I know. Michael's in Florida right now so we talk a lot on the phone. Eddie's in Vegas so we are together each week. For example, last week just before Christmas, Eddie and I went shopping for a gift for his current girlfriend. **It seems serious so I have bothered to learn her name.** I tried not to clutter my brain cells with his previous girlfriends since they tended not to last and it was always awkward when I would meet them and call them the wrong name! At any rate, I think the current one hates it when Eddie and I go shopping. If she had to put it into words, it would go like this: **"Charlie will find something really weird, Eddie will like it and buy it, and I'll have to wear it or see it for the rest of my life!"** So as not to dis-appoint her, we went to a Swap Meet in Vegas last Wednesday and I found a statue of a pair of skeletons dressed as a bride and groom holding a sign that reads: **"Love Never Dies."** I found it, Eddie liked it and bought it, and I can only imagine his girlfriend's joy when she opened it on Christmas! And since he wanted another gift to give her, we kept looking and stopped at this weapons stand in the swap meet. They had a really cool knife disguised as a lipstick holder. I liked that, but Eddie found a miniature stun gun which he liked better so we bought that for her. **I can hardly wait to hear about the first time she uses 300,000 volts on Eddie.** Ah, I love hanging out with my illegitimate son!

The Christmas holidays always bring a certain amount of nostalgia. Like many other folks I know, I call up or visit old friends. I even pull out some of the old photo albums. Maybe it's just the joy of seeing myself with lots of dark brown hair, or maybe it's the wonderful memories of the past. Whatever it is, it is good to be reminded of the old ties of family and friends, of the times spent together, of the lessons learned. Oh, we all have relatives and friends that are a little **"unique"**, but that's what makes life so interesting. It drives some of my relatives crazy that I have a two signs I love. One reads: **"God gave us our relatives...thank God we can choose our friends!"** The other reads: **"Friends are God's apology for giving us families!"** So very true sometimes....

There aren't any photographs of Jesus and Mary and Joseph at home in Nazareth, or at any other time in Jesus' life. Imagine what the home movies and old photos of Jesus' family would have shown us. Jesus as a child sitting with Mary, or working in the family carpenter shop with Joseph, or playing outside with His friends. **(Now, there's a fascinating thought....Jesus must have had friends when He was growing up.)** Or think of the pictures that would have shown Jesus and His family visiting the Temple in Jerusalem or growing up in Nazareth. Thirty years went by in Nazareth, and Jesus grew into the Man whose life and teachings would change the whole world.

SOMETHING HAPPENED AT NAZARETH, something happened in Jesus' home and surroundings. When Jesus left Nazareth to begin His mission as Savior of the world, He was a man of incredible power - the power to heal, to console, to forgive, to save.

SOMETHING HAPPENED AT NAZARETH that helped Jesus become the Man for others that Matthew, Mark, Luke and John would later write about in their Gospels; the Man that made Paul see us as chosen members of the Lord's own family who should imitate His own forgiveness and patience and kindness towards others. We may not have pictures of what happened at Nazareth, but we sure do have some very strong testimony that whatever happened there during those thirty formative years helped to make Jesus into a Man who would one day lay down His own life for the salvation of the world.

I wonder how many times in the course of His life Jesus must have thought back to those years in Nazareth, those people He knew and loved. I like to think Jesus drew a lot of strength from those relationships with Mary and Joseph and His extended family and friends.

As we honor the Holy Family today, as we think about those thirty years at Nazareth, we might want to also think about our own families, our own friends, our own home towns now. Are we clothed with mercy and kindness? Can we forgive and bear with one another? Are we peaceful and thankful? Are these the memories our families and friends will carry into life in the years ahead?

SOMETHING HAPPENED AT NAZARETH, something wonderful. Something is happening in our homes too. May it be something wonderful too. Years from now, I hope we can all look back and remember that **SOMETHING HAPPENED HERE IN PARADISE** that changed our lives for the better too.

God bless you!

Farrell Dillon, One of the Brightest Young
Magicians I know!

Michael Turco, Another of the Brightest
Young Magicians I Know!

Mary, the Mother of God

1 January 2010

FIRST READING: Numbers 6:22-27
PSALM: Psalm 67:2-3, 5-6, 8
SECOND READING: Galatians 4:4-7
GOSPEL: Luke 2:16-21

If Mary is the Mother of Jesus, and if Jesus really is God, then Mary is really the Mother of God.

Today we honor Mary as the Mother of God. It's her oldest title...dating back to the Council of Ephesus in 431 A.D. Because Mary is the Mother of Jesus, and because Jesus is God, Mary can rightly be called the Mother of God. So we Catholics honor Mary because of her relationship with God.

A famous Christian writer, Max Lucado, developed a list of 25 questions that he would like to ask Mary when he gets to heaven. I'll just mention a few of them for us to think about today as we honor Mary, the Mother of God. They are really interesting to think about:

What was it like watching Jesus pray?

When He saw a rainbow, did He ever mention a flood?

Did you ever feel awkward teaching Him how He created the world?

Did the thought ever occur to you that the God to Whom you were praying was asleep under your roof?

What did He and His cousin John talk about as kids?

Did He have any friends named Judas?

Did you ever think That's God eating my soup?

To start the new year, let me tell you one little story that I found on the Internet...

A certain king had two servants. To the first he said: **"I want you to travel for a year throughout my kingdom and bring back a sample of every weed you can find."** To the second servant, the king said: **"I want you to travel for a year throughout my kingdom and bring back a sample of every flower you can find."** One year later, both servants stood before the king. To the first, the king asked: **"Have you carried out my command?"** And the first servant answered: **"I have, and I was amazed to find there were so many weeds in your kingdom. In fact, there is nothing but weeds in this kingdom."** To the king's question, the second servant also answered: **"I have, and I was amazed to find there were so many incredible flowers in your kingdom. In fact, there are nothing but beautiful flowers in this kingdom."**

These two servants each found what they were looking for. And so do we.

Are there no blessings in your life.....or is your life full of blessings?

Do you have no one who loves you.....or is more love being offered that you could imagine?

Is there no beauty outside your windows.....or it is just waiting there for you to see and appreciate it?

Is there no strength left in your body.....or do you have strength from God that you haven't used?

Are there no new pleasures or opportunities.....or are they waiting just outside you door?

Do you have no faith or peace or love left.....or are they just waiting for you to draw upon them?

Like the two servants, we will find in this new year what we are looking for. There is more good than evil in the world. There always has been, and there always will be. Just look for it, and you will find it.

The Lord bless you and keep you.

The Lord let His face shine upon you and be gracious to you.

The Lord look upon you and give you peace.

May you have a blessed and a happy new year in
2010.

God bless you!

Nick Mulpagano as Elvis!

The Epiphany of the Lord

3 January 2010

FIRST READING: Isaiah 60:1-6
PSALM: Psalm 72:1-2, 7-8, 10-11, 12-13
SECOND READING: Ephesians 3:2-3, 5-6
GOSPEL: Matthew 2:1-12

In this new year 2010, may we always recognize and appreciate the gifts that God gives us.

Welcome to the first Sunday of the new year here in Paradise! Weather here still beats out New Jersey's winters by a lot. I really want to thank everyone who made Christmas so beautiful here at St. John's. I'm really proud to report that over 1500 people celebrated Christmas with us last week, almost the same identical number as last year. And I'm astounded to report that even in this economy, our Christmas collection reached another all-time high! Last year, we received just about $13,600.00 which was more than double what we had ever received before. This Christmas, we received over $15,500.00 - nearly $2000.00 more than last year. Your generosity is incredible! **So THANK YOU, THANK YOU, AND THANK YOU AGAIN to our residents and to our visitors.**

I had a wonderful Christmas, and so far have over a dozen fruitcakes to eat. I hope no one ever discovers that fruitcake is bad for your health! After all, fruit is supposed to be good for you!

I finally started reading my Christmas cards and emails, and I found this beautiful sentiment from my friend Dustin, who is a really well-known video editor in Hollywood: **"Charlie, I hope to be as happy as you are if God chooses to keep me here that long. I never wanted to get old, but you make it sound like your life just began in Nevada. What's your secret?"**

My friends Paul and Charlie and I celebrated our first anniversary of knowing each other by going out for lunch on December 30th up in Vegas just like we had done last year. We had such a good time that we decided to make it an annual event - same place, same date, every year. They're both younger than I am so when we were leaving, Paul said to me: **"You're older than we are so don't you go spoiling our fun for next year by dying on us!"** Now there's a cheery thought for the new year from my friends! I'll have to try not to die so as not to spoil their fun!

My Internet friends have not forgotten me during the Christmas Season, and my email box has been filling up each day. Among the best items I have received comes from my friend, Diane, in South Jersey who shared the following item with me entitled: **GIFT WRAPPING TIPS FOR MEN**.

This is the time of year when we think back to the very first Christmas, when the Three Wise Men went to see the Baby Jesus and, according to the Book of Matthew, **"presented unto Him gifts of gold, frankincense and myrrh."** These are simple words, but if we analyze them carefully we discover an important, yet often overlooked, theological fact: **There is no mention of wrapping paper**. If there had been wrapping paper, Matthew would have said so: **"And lo, the gifts were inside 600 square cubits of paper. And the paper was festooned with pictures of Frosty the Snowman. And Joseph was going to throweth it away, but Mary saideth unto him, she saideth 'Holdeth it! That is nice paper! Saveth it for next year!' And Joseph did rolleth his eyeballs. And the Baby Jesus was more interested in the paper than in the frankincense."**

But these words **DO NOT** appear in the Bible, which means that the very first Christmas gifts were **NOT** wrapped. This is because the people giving those gifts had two important characteristics: 1. They were wise. 2. They were men. Men are not big gift wrappers. Men do not understand the point of putting paper on a gift just so somebody else can tear it off. This is not just my opinion. This is a scientific fact based on a statistical survey of two guys I know. One is Rob, who said that the only time he ever wraps a gift is "If it's such a poor gift that I don't want to be there when the person opens it." The other is Gene, who told me he does wrap gifts, but as a matter of principle never takes more than 15 seconds per gift. "No one ever had to wonder which presents Daddy wrapped at Christmas," Gene said, "They were always the ones that looked like enormous spitballs."

I also wrap gifts, but because of some defect in my motor skills, I can never completely wrap them. I can take a gift the size of a deck of cards and put it in the exact center of a piece of wrapping paper the size of a regulation volleyball court, but when I am done folding and taping, you can still see a section of the gift peeking out. (Sometimes I camouflage this section with a marking pen.) On the other hand, if you give most women a 12 inch square of wrapping paper, they can wrap a C-130 cargo plane. One of my female friends actually like wrapping things. If she gives you a gift that requires batteries, she wraps the batteries separately, which to me is very close to being a symptom of mental illness. If it were possible, I think she would wrap each individual volt!

So today, I am presenting GIFT-WRAPPING TIPS FOR MEN:

1. Whenever possible, buy gifts that are already wrapped. If, when the recipient opens the gift, neither one of you recognizes it, you can claim that it's myrrh.

2. The editors of Woman's Day magazine recently ran an item on how to make your own wrapping paper

by printing a design on it with an apple sliced in half horizontally and dipped in a mixture of food coloring and liquid starch. They must be smoking drugs!

3. If you're giving a hard-to-wrap gift, skip the wrapping paper! Just put it inside a bag and stick one of those little adhesive bows on it. This creates a festive visual effect that is sure to delight the lucky recipient on Christmas morning.

YOUR WIFE: Why is there a Hefty trash bag under the tree?

YOU: It's a gift! See, it has a bow!

YOUR WIFE:(peering into the trash bag): It's a leaf blower!

YOU: Yeah! Gas-powered! Five horsepower!

YOUR WIFE: Get out of here!

YOU: I also got you some myrrh.

As we celebrate Epiphany this year, as we remember this Christmas and the Christmases of our past, as we look forward to the new year 2010 which opens before us, I just want to say a couple of things:

This is truly the year the Lord is giving to us. As the Prophet Isaiah says in the first reading: **"Your light has come, the glory of the Lord shines on you."**

During this new year 2010, there are some people in our lives now who will not be there next year, **APPRECIATE THEM NOW - SHARE WHAT YOU HAVE WITH THEM NOW - TELL THEM THAT YOU CARE ABOUT THEM NOW.** Don't put off that kind word or that kind action. Say it or do it now! Take the time to live, to love, and to laugh **NOW** in 2010.

During this new year 2010, some people will enter our lives who had not been there before, they will come in through births, adoptions, marriages, friendships, **WELCOME THEM NOW - BE OPEN TO WHATEVER WONDERS THEY CAN BRING INTO YOUR LIVES NOW - APPRECIATE THE LESSONS THEY CAN TEACH YOU NOW in 2010.**

Right here and right now, we are the people that God in His eternal plan has put into our places, into our families, into our jobs, into our schools, into our parishes, among our friends. This is the gift of the present moment! Don't miss out on it!

In conclusion, to go back to some opening comments on gifts, remember that the important thing is not what you give, or how you wrap it. The important thing, now and throughout the new year, is to recognize the gifts and miracles that God places into our lives day after day, and to resolve to pay attention to what God is doing.

God bless you!

Ben Stone and Jasmine Trias.....What a Great Couple!

The Baptism of the Lord

10 January 2010

FIRST READING: Isaiah 42:1-4, 6-7
PSALM: Psalm 29:1-4, 9-10
SECOND READING: Acts 10:34-38
GOSPEL: Luke 3:15-16, 21-22

Every Baptism celebrates the fact that one more person is being joined to the life, death and resurrection of Jesus.

Another great week in Laughlin! Have you ever noticed how beautiful it is here? I keep taking pictures. Tourists travel hundreds of miles to see what I get to see every day! My friends in NJ have started referring to Laughlin as **"Paradise"** when they write or call me because I've told them so much about it. Now I intend to spend eternity in the real Paradise, but until then, Laughlin comes pretty close! I'm still enjoying the remnants of Christmas cookies and the remaining fruitcakes. Somehow I managed to have eggplant parmegiana (which I love!) two times this week! And a great stuffed flounder up in Vegas at a restaurant with the tables set up around a huge fish tank. The only problem was that the fish in the tank kept staring at me while I was eating!

My friend Flash is in town so I got no sleep up in Vegas this week. Getting to bed at 3:00 AM or later for a few days definitely takes its toll! When I got back to Laughlin, I made a stop at the hospital to see some of our parishioners there. One of the volunteers looked at me and told me that I have a **"wonderful twinkle"** in my eye! I told her that it's not a **"twinkle"**, it's just me being bleary-eyed from lack of sleep! Flash is a magician and is looking for a house in Vegas so we found one on Magical View Street. Think it might be perfect. It'd be a cool envelope to address: **FLASH at Magical View Street, Las Vegas!**

Besides living in Paradise and seeing Vegas every week, one of the other things I like about being a priest is baptizing babies. I've baptized almost 600 babies! And these ceremonies are always exciting. You never know what the baby will do when suddenly he/she is confronted with a strange man pouring cool water over his/her head. But as much as I love the ceremony itself, I love the preparation time with first-time parents even more. For parents, as well as for their children, Baptism is often a new beginning of Faith. Becoming a mother and a father sometimes brings a couple back to practicing the Faith they are asking to be given to their child. It does make sense.... after all, why would you want to have your child baptized into a Faith that you yourself don't bother to practice?

I love the blessing of the baptismal water. We take plain Laughlin tap water and bless it with a lengthy blessing that recalls a number of occasions when

God has used water in the past to achieve some purpose or miracle. I usually ask the parents what examples of this they might recall hearing about in the Bible. Sometimes I have to prod them to remember what they have heard. I had one class where a parent remembered Jesus washing the Apostles' feet with water on Holy Thursday. I said "**GREAT!** Now think of something in the Bible with **MORE WATER!**" So someone remembered Jesus turning gallons of water into wine at the wedding feast in Cana. I said "**THINK OF MORE WATER**".....and someone remembered Jesus' own baptism in the Jordan River (which we commemorate today).... and I said"**THINK OF EVEN MORE WATER**"...and someone remembered Moses leading the Israelites across the Red Sea out of slavery into freedom. I said, "You're missing one really big event with a **WHOLE LOT OF WATER!**" But no one got it. Finally I gave a hint: **"BIG BOAT"**. And someone remembered Noah and the Ark when God cleansed the whole earth with water.

Why make such a big thing about a blessing of water? Because at every Baptism, Jesus continues to work wonders with water. It is no less a miracle than the crossing of the Red Sea, or the changing of water into wine, or the cleansing of the whole earth at the time of Noah, that God Himself would bring creatures like us into His kingdom for all eternity. **But that in fact is what Baptism does.** When we are baptized, we begin the process by which we will develop in the Catholic Faith and eventually,

God willing, inherit eternal life with God. **Each Baptism is the beginning of an eternal miracle. And it is a step towards eternity in the real Paradise.**

All of us who have been baptized have been brought into a relationship with God that will last for all eternity. As we celebrate today the Baptism of Jesus, I just thought it would be good to remind you how fortunate we are to have been baptized. Isaiah puts it very well in today's First Reading: **"I, THE LORD, HAVE CALLED YOU; I HAVE GRASPED YOU BY THE HAND."** Just think of that image for a moment......you and I are walking hand-in-hand with God! Doesn't that make you feel really secure? When things get really tough as they sometimes do in life, you can reach out and God's hand will be there to steady you and support you.

As we continue our journey through life, may we never forget how close God has chosen to be to us. May we keep our hands safely in His throughout our lives. What began at our baptism goes on into eternity. **How fortunate we are to be holding hands with God!**

God bless you!

Practicing my sleeper hold!

2nd Sunday in Ordinary Time - "C"

17 January 2010

FIRST READING: Isaiah 62:1-5
PSALM: Psalm 96:1-3, 7-10
SECOND READING: 1 Corinthians 12:4-11
GOSPEL: John 2:1-11

All those waiters at that wedding in Cana knew that the wine had run out. They also knew that Jesus had done something about it.

Laughlin still remains warmer than New Jersey, and that will always be a good thing especially in the winter! I get a fiendish thrill out of calling or emailing friends back there and telling them our temperatures! It must be my evil dark side coming out! We got a nice plug for the parish up in Las Vegas last week. I was at Lance Burton's show and he announced that my birthday is coming up and then recommended if people are coming to Laughlin, they should really come and see St. John the Baptist Catholic Church when they're here. So now there are 1200 more people who know about us. I hope they don't all come at once! Lance is coming up on 50 years old himself this year, so he continued to joke with the audience that he's younger than me! I guess that's his dark side coming out. But then he took me out to dinner, so it's okay.

Speaking of getting older, two elderly ladies met for the first time since high school. One asked the other, **"You were always so organized in school, meticulously planning every detail. Did you plan your married life as carefully?"** Her friend replied, **"Yes, just as carefully. My first husband was a millionaire, my second husband was an actor, my third husband was a preacher, and now I'm married to an undertaker."** Her friend asked, **"What do those marriages have to do with a meticulously planned life? You married a millioniare, then an actor, then a preacher, and now an undertaker."** And the first woman replied, **"One for the money, two for the show, three to get ready, and four to go."**

There are a lot of jokes about weddings, but weddings are serious moments in life. Today's Gospel is about a wedding celebration. And it's worth thinking about it a little.

Years ago on the old TONIGHT SHOW, Johnny Carson was interviewing an eight-year-old boy one night. The young boy was asked to appear on the Late Show because he had rescued two friends from a coal mine outside his hometown in West Virginia. As Johnny questioned him, it became apparent that the boy was a Christian, so Johnny asked him if he attended Sunday School. The boy said he did, so Johnny inquired **"What are you learning in Sunday School?"** The boy said, **"Last week our lesson was about how Jesus went to a wedding with his**

mother, and turned water into wine." Johnny then asked, **"Well, what did you learn from that story?"** And the boy squirmed in his chair. It was obvious that he hadn't thought about that. But then he lifted up his face and said, **"I guess if you're going to have a wedding, make sure you invite Jesus and Mary!"** And that is precisely the message of today's Gospel. **Make sure you invite Jesus and Mary wherever you live and wherever you go.** They are the ones who can really help you.

And it is really interesting to note that: "Do whatever He tells you" is the only piece of advice given by Mary recorded in the New Testament. So it's likely to be good for us to remember that.

I think it's also good for us to know that Jesus celebrated events in people's lives, He went to parties. In fact, He worked His first miracle at a wedding party. So in honor of the wedding feast at Cana in today's Gospel, instead of a sermon, I'd like to propose a toast!

TO ALL THOSE WHO WORK TO PROMOTE THE SANCTITY OF HUMAN LIFE....to all those who remind us that life is sacred from the moment of conception. To all those dedicated firefighters, police, and rescue squad workers who protect all of us. To all those doctors and nurses and healthcare workers who care for the sick. To all those servicemen and women who risk their lives deployed around the world so we can live in safety.

TO ALL THOSE WHO WORK TO PROMOTE CHRISTIAN UNITY AND RACIAL HARMONY....as we recall Christian Unity Week and the birthday of Martin Luther King, Jr. this month.

TO ALL THOSE WAITERS AT THE WEDDING FEAST OF CANA in today's Gospel....whose names are unknown to us, but who were the first to witness Jesus' power. Imagine how they felt that day! They knew they had filled those water jars with **WATER**, perhaps 150 gallons of it. And they knew that because of Jesus, it wasn't **WATER** any more. Imagine their enthusiasm and perhaps their frustration as they tried to share what they knew with their families and friends when they got home that night!

TO ALL OF US, THE PARISHIONERS and VISITORS HERE AT ST. JOHN THE BAPTIST....as we begin this new year, and as we catch a glimpse of Jesus' power at work in today's Gospel. May we be as excited and as enthusiastic as those waiters must have been! **After all, we see a miracle here every Sunday when bread and wine become the BODY and BLOOD of Jesus Christ. That should thrill us!**

May we realize that Jesus still lives and still has power to change not only water into wine, or bread and wine into His own BODY and BLOOD, but also hatred into love, fear into hope, and sinners into saints. We just have to remember to invite Jesus and Mary, and then be willing to do whatever they tell us.

God bless you!

Jacob Jax, cool and classy!

3rd Sunday in Ordinary Time - "C"

24 January 2010

FIRST READING: Nehemiah 8:2-6, 8-10
PSALM: Psalm 19:8-10, 15
SECOND READING: 1 Corinthians 12:12-30
GOSPEL: Luke 1:1-4; 4:14-21

At its heart, true religion is really magical!

What a rainy week! Deacon Dan and I were in Palm Springs from Monday through Thursday at the Clergy Education Week. Didn't get to see much of the town because of the pouring rain and it took us nearly 7 hours to drive back to Laughlin on Thursday. We forded some raging waters along the way! I kept hoping the bishop was stuck in a flood somewhere heading home to Las Vegas so that maybe next year he wouldn't have the education week so far away from Paradise! The conference was good. And the topic was medical ethics. One speaker was a really organized teacher whom I thoroughly enjoyed. The other speaker had great material but lacked organization. I wanted to run up, knock him out, grab his notes and organize them so I could give them back to him when he regained consciousness. But I stayed in my seat. Since we were staying at an Indian Casino, I tried my luck late one night on a Happy Days slot machine and got 78 free spins with a 12 times multiplier winning $423.00. The next morning, Bishop Pepe congratulated me on the win. I asked him how he knew about it, and he told me he has his ways. I can't remember the last time a bishop had congratulated me on a slot machine win! And I found this awesome Jewish Deli next to the hotel so I ended up eating there a few times. Great potato pancakes, and thick sandwiches on awesome rye bread with kosher pickles. I tried to put into action the words from today's First Reading: **"Go, eat rich foods and drink sweet drinks...Do not be saddened this day, for rejoicing in the Lord must be your strength."**

Got back to Laughlin on Thursday in time for the Rat Pack show at the Riverside. I'm old enough to remember the original Rat Pack, so it was a super trip down Memory Lane to see the show. Besides the music, I loved the comedy of the Joey Bishop impersonator. Might have to steal some of his material for later in the year. And I have to show off one of my birthday gifts.....I got this really cool hat so now I can kind of magically have spiked hair whenever I want.

I didn't get to see any magic shows in Palm Springs, but you know I always try to find them in Vegas or here in Laughlin. I turned 62 years old last Tuesday, and the older I get, the more I realize there really is magic in the world. Oh, it's not just the magic that is on the stages of Laughlin and Las Vegas (as great as that magic is), but it's the magic that leads one person to care about another person. It's the magic that leads an old married couple to take care of each other and support each other even when sickness takes away some of their freedom. It's the magic that shines in a young couple's eyes on their wedding day as they pledge their love from that day forward no matter what the future might hold for them. It's the magic of friends watching out for each other and making sure no one is left out of a game, and no one has to face things all alone. It's the magic of those who have something to share being willing to share it with others: parents with children, teachers with students, friends with each other.

At its very heart, I believe, that **true religion is really magical**. It introduces us to a world beyond ourselves, to a world larger and brighter and more hopeful and exciting than we can imagine. Today's Scripture readings speak of that magic. In the First Reading, just hearing the words of the Law of God, brings the people to weep for joy as they are told to rejoice in the Lord and to share what they have. The Second Reading from St. Paul's Letter to the Corinthians reminds us we are all connected, we are like parts of the same body. We are supposed to build up the body in holiness by using our God-given gifts for each other. And finally, in the Gospel of St. Luke, Jesus tells us He has come to proclaim liberty, healing and strength to those in need.

True religion enables us to see the world as a magical place, a place where each person is important because each person is created by God, a place where miracles can and do happen in the hearts and minds of the people as well as in their physical bodies, a place where God continues to reveal Himself and share Himself with us, His people. **I honestly feel sorry for those people who lack religion or who see it as something that should make people feel sad or guilty.** True religion opens our minds and hearts and eyes to a world of magic, a world of possibilities, a world still being created by God, a world in which God places each one of us where we can do the most good and where we can find the greatest satisfaction.

I don't ask that you see the world through rose-colored glasses, or that you ignore it's defects and imperfections. Lord knows they are many and can be really burdensome. But I do ask that you open your eyes and minds and hearts to see the beauty and the magic happening right in front of you every day in so many ways. **Try to look at the world as God sees it, and see the magic of God.** May you feel His power and His presence every day of your lives. Nothing will make you feel better or more holy than seeing God working with you in your world each day. Because this is not just my world, or your world, this is God's world. **Amazing things happen here. Don't miss any of them!**

God bless you!

A Visit to Oatman, AZ!

4th Sunday in Ordinary Time - "C"

31 January 2010

FIRST READING: Jeremiah 1:4-5, 17-19
PSALM: Psalm 71:1-6, 15, 17
SECOND READING: 1 Corinthians 12:31-13:13
GOSPEL: Luke 4:21-30

Love is patient and love is kind.

Well, the rain is finally gone from Paradise! I'm told that we're going to have a beautiful spring in the desert because of all the extra water. It was a great week for eating thanks to some wonderful corn/vegetable enchiladas with lots of cheese showing up in my office, along with some banana bread, chocolate-covered almonds, cookies, cinnamon buns, and a great sandwich of sliced mozzarella with tomatoes, onions and a little balsamic vinegar on a bun. And there were two wonderful food-related events in Laughlin this week: the dedication of the new Colorado River Food Bank which does so much good for our community, and the monthly mixer for the Laughlin Chamber of Commerce which featured an awesome selection of foods at the Riverside on Friday night. Thanks to Janet from the Laughlin Chamber of Commerce, I found myself on stage with a group of people about to be hypnotized during the event. I tried, but just didn't go under his spell. I kept thinking about the story of the hypnotist who went to entertain the people at a local nursing home. He tried to put them under using his grandfather's pocket watch which he swung back and forth in front of them after telling them how valuable the watch was to him. Suddenly he accidently dropped the watch, breaking it into hundreds of little pieces. It startled him so much that he just yelled **"Crap!"** ... and it took them several weeks to clean up the nursing home. Also got up to Vegas to see Wayne Newton's show and was surprised to discover that he has groupies. There was one woman at my table who nearly passed out when Wayne came over and touched her hands. The show was good, but I didn't even come close to passing out. Much more enjoyable was seeing Dixie Dooley's magic show featuring Harvey, a 20 pound German giant rabbit. There were lots of kids at the show, but I waited patiently in line with them so I could pet the rabbit at the end of the show. You just don't get to see a 20 pound, 3 foot long rabbit every day!

Last weekend, I told you I really believe true religion is really magical because it introduces us to a world beyond ourselves, to a world larger and brighter and more hopeful and exciting than we can imagine. Today's Scripture readings speak of that same magic. In the First Reading, the Prophet Jeremiah is told that God has formed him even before his birth, and will always be with him. What a powerful statement! God has chosen us even before we were born! He knows about each one of us. He cares for each one of us. And in the

Gospel today from St. Luke, we hear about the beginning of Jesus' preaching about the salvation and help He came into the world to bring. But it is the Second Reading from St. Paul's Letter to the Corinthians that is the most powerful today. It is a reading that reminds us of most of the weddings we've ever attended. It speaks powerfully of **LOVE** being an action that we all need to do. **Love is patient (so you and I need to be patient), love is kind (so you and I need to do things that are kind).** I've always thought that particular reading is neglected because we only use it at weddings, when it really should be something we think about every day. In fact, I'd like to try something with you today to drive that point home. I'm going to read each line of it, and I want you to repeat it **OUT LOUD** after me. Then we're going to read each line again, but this time instead of saying the word LOVE, we're going to insert our own first names when we repeat it. Don't be shy, we're all here among friends. Here goes.....

Love is patient. **LOVE IS PATIENT.**
Charlie is patient. ____**IS PATIENT.**

Love is kind. **LOVE IS KIND.**
Charlie is kind. ____**IS KIND.**
Love is not jealous. **LOVE IS NOT JEALOUS.**
Charlie is not jealous. ____**IS NOT JEALOUS.**

Love is not pompous. **LOVE IS NOT POMPOUS.**
Charlie is not pompous. ____**IS NOT POMPOUS.**

Love is not inflated. **LOVE IS NOT INFLATED.**
Charlie is not inflated. ____ **IS NOT INFLATED.**

Love is not rude. **LOVE IS NOT RUDE.**
Charlie is not rude. ____**IS NOT RUDE.**

Love is not quick-tempered. **LOVE IS NOT QUICK-TEMPERED.**
Charlie is not quick-tempered. ____**IS NOT QUICK-TEMPERED.**

Love does not brood over injuries. **LOVE DOES NOT BROOD OVER INJURIES.**
Charlie does not brood over injuries. ____ **DOES NOT BROOD OVER INJURIES.**

Love does not rejoice over wrongdoing. **LOVE DOES NOT REJOICE OVER WRONGDOING.**
Charlie does not rejoice over wrongdoing. ____ **DOES NOT REJOICE OVER WRONGDOING.**

Love bears all things. **LOVE BEARS ALL THINGS.**
Charlie bears all things. ____ **BEARS ALL THINGS.**

Love believes all things. **LOVE BELIEVES ALL THINGS.**
Charlie believes all things. ____ **BELIEVES ALL THINGS.**

Love hopes all things. **LOVE HOPES ALL THINGS.**
Charlie hopes all things. ____**HOPES ALL THINGS.**

Love endures all things. **LOVE ENDURES ALL THINGS.**
Charlie endures all things. ____**ENDURES ALL THINGS.**

Love never fails. **LOVE NEVER FAILS.**
Charlie never fails. ____ **NEVER FAILS.**

So how did you feel saying your own name in all those places where there should be love? Sometimes I felt like a hypocrite, sometimes I felt really good, sometimes I felt like I could be doing a lot better to make my statements true. How do you fit into this reading? When did you feel like a hypocrite? When did you feel really good? When did you feel that you could be doing a lot better to make your statements true? Think about it this week.

God bless you!

5th Sunday in Ordinary Time - "C"

7 February 2010

FIRST READING: Isaiah 6:1-8
PSALM: Psalm 138:1-5, 7-8
SECOND READING: 1 Corinthians 15:1-11
GOSPEL: Luke 5:1-11

Are you ready for what God is asking you to do for Him this week?

Well, it sure is good to be here in Paradise! New Jersey and much of the East Coast is getting slammed with a major snowstorm this weekend, and here we are in short-sleeve shirts!

This was another great week for eating with some awesome garlic mashed potatoes and lots of shrimp on Friday night at a local casino, and even a piece of homemade chocolate fruitcake - what a super combination - chocolate and fruitcake all in one!

I went for a haircut this week and explained that I wanted it left long on the top and really short on the sides and neck. When she got finished, the stylist asked one of the other customers if I looked like Bart Simpson!

Wednesday was the Feast of St. Blaise so after Mass this weekend, we will bless the throats of everyone who would like to have that blessing. You may not know it, but every year a group of sword-swallowers in Las Vegas go to the Guardian Angel Cathedral on St. Blaise's Day to get their throats blessed! Most of us are not sticking sharp objects down our throats, but the blessing is still a beautiful and prayerful occasion.

And I got to play Super Mario Car Racing with Eddie on our new Wii this week. After we played for awhile, and I lost to him every time, he asked if I wanted to play against some people around the world. So we set up the race and found 10 other people online to join in. So there I sat with my little steering wheel in hand battling folks around the world in a car race. And I'm pleased to report that I came in at #10. I actually managed to beat two guys in England! Of course, I don't know how old they were, they might have been 4 year old kids, but I still beat them! A win is a win!

And speaking of wins....**this is Super Bowl weekend.** And I'm ready for it! For Christmas, one of our parishioners gave me this really cool book - **FOOTBALL FOR DUMMIES** - so I can learn all about the game. And on page 292, it explains that the game was originally called the AFL-NFL World Championship Game. But the new name - SUPER BOWL - was coined for the 1969 game by Kansas City Chiefs owner Lamar Hunt. He got the idea for the name from a new toy that year - the Super Ball - which had super bouncing abilities. See how much I've learned from FOOTBALL FOR DUMMIES already! This year the Super Bowl is between the Colts and the Saints. I was going to ask our cantor to lead us in singing WHEN THE SAINTS GO MARCHING IN today, but figured we better avoid it in case there are some COLTS fans in the congregation! **But I have to cheer for the SAINTS to win! I don't want people going around saying that the priest in Laughlin is against the SAINTS!**

Today is an anniversary for me. 19 years ago, 7 February 1991, I was notified that I had been mobilized by the Air Force as part of Operation Desert Storm, and 8 days later, the day after Valentine's Day, I reported to Dover AFB in Delaware. I was one of the lucky ones. I was given 8 days to get ready. Some of my AF friends received only a few days notice. One of my friends, Tom Malloy, received only 24 hours notice. I met up with him during the war, and of course I asked him what he did during those 24 hours. What things were on his mind as he prepared to leave his wife and 4 children. He said there were two things he had to do: he had to get a power of attorney written and signed for his wife, Donna. And he had to teach her how to run the lawn mower. **"I don't want to come home from the war to a messed-up lawn!"**

I mention Desert Storm today for two reasons: **ONE**, the world situation today certainly finds more than a few parallels with that experience of 19 years ago, and certainly we should be offering our prayers not only for peace in the Middle East, but for those soldiers, sailors, airmen, marines and coast guardsmen who put their lives on the line every day for us. And **TWO**, because I think there is something really important in today's First Reading from the Prophet Isaiah that kind of parallels the experience of God we all have. During Desert Storm, many of us compared stories of how our lives and work had been affected, and we discovered a lot of similarities. I think the same is true of the story of ISAIAH'S call as a prophet. It was a pivotal experience that in some way is repeated in the lives of all of us who come to know and serve the Lord. **Isaiah's story is also our story.** Let me explain what I mean:

There are 4 things that happen in that brief passage:

1. Isaiah has an experience of God's presence. The Lord is seated on a high and lofty throne, dressed like a king, larger than life, surrounded by angels crying out how holy God is. Everyone of us has some image, some vision of God. It might be the same as Isaiah's - God is King - or it might be a little different - God is a Friend, or God is a Teacher, or God is a Judge. But all of us relate to God in some way, and we have some visual way in which we think of Him, and we have some experience of Him in our lives.

2. The experience of God reminds Isaiah of his own sinfulness, his own unworthiness to be near God. **"WOE IS ME, I AM DOOMED! I AM A MAN OF UNCLEAN LIPS!"** As we draw closer to God, we become much more aware of our own sinfulness.

Think of the way you look and smell when you've been outside working in the yard. You don't seem to notice it much at the time. But just walk

inside and get near someone who is not sweaty and smelly and dirty...it won't take you long to realize your situation.

3. Isaiah is forgiven, and he never forgot it! A huge angel with a burning piece of charcoal came and pressed it to Isaiah's lips saying: **"YOUR WICKEDNESS IS REMOVED, YOUR SIN IS PURGED!"** Hey, if I saw a gigantic angel flying up to me with a flaming piece of charcoal, I'd be pretty impressed myself! The forgiveness that we receive in the Sacrament of Confession might be less dramatic, but it is not less real and no less unforgetable.

4. And finally, having come close to God, having realized his own unworthiness, and having experienced God's forgiveness, Isaiah is now ready to respond when God asks: **"WHOM SHALL I SEND?"** and Isaiah responds **"HERE I AM, SEND ME!"**

As you and I draw closer to God in prayer and faithfulness to His teachings and His Church, we too realize how completely unworthy we are of God's attention and care. But if we take that next step and approach God for His forgiveness in Confession and in our prayers and actions, we will definitely feel God's forgiveness as powerfully as Isaiah did. And then, and this is the best part, and then you and I will be ready to respond to whatever God is calling us to do.

This week, think about Isaiah and his experiences in today's First Reading. And then compare Isaiah's experience with your own life. How do you picture God? Have you felt His power and forgiveness in your life?   Are you ready for what God is asking you to do for Him this week? When God calls, are you ready to respond with Isaiah: **"HERE I AM, SEND ME?"**

God bless you!

Joseph, a Really, Really Good Friend!

6th Sunday in Ordinary Time - "C"

14 February 2010

FIRST READING: Jeremiah 17:5-8
PSALM: Psalm 1:1-4, 6
SECOND READING: 1 Corinthians 15:12, 16-20
GOSPEL: Luke 6:17, 20-26

We draw our life from Christ, Our Savior.

The Smothers Brothers are in town this week. Back in 1995, when they were appearing at the Riverside, I had written them a letter saying that my Mom and I would be coming to visit Laughlin that weekend and would there be any way I could get to meet them. I grew up with them on TV. I told them I had tickets for their Saturday night show. I never heard back from them, but when we went to the show, they did a skit about telling a lie. And it was near Washington's birthday, so Dick stopped Tommy and said, **"You're lying to all these people! How can you do that when it's George Washington's Birthday who never told a lie?** They played around with it for awhile and then Dick said, **"I've invited Father Charlie backstage to hear your confession."** Well, I took it as a hint, and after the show, Mom and I went backstage, and sure enough got to meet them. They said they knew I'd be at the show on Saturday, so they would just make it part of the show. It was fun seeing them again this week, right back here at the Riverside where I had met them 15 years ago.

Another great week here in Paradise! Last Friday I discovered an interesting item.....there was snow on the ground of 49 out of the 50 states. Hawaii was the only state without some snow! And fortunately, Laughlin had none either! We are so fortunate to be living here or visiting here! And it's Valentine's Day weekend....so I printed some interesting quotations about love in the bulletin. Be sure to check them out. If I were younger, some of them would be great pick-up lines! My personal favorite is a thought about Valentine's Day: **"I don't understand why Cupid was chosen to represent Valentine's Day. When I think about romance, the last thing on my mind is a short, chubby toddler coming at me with a weapon."** And even though I love to write, I can't send you all a Valentine's Day card, but I certainly do wish you all an awesome Valentine's Day. In my mind, few days could be better than one devoted to love and chocolate!

Speaking of writing, I discovered a really interesting bit of historical trivia concerning Tuesday of this week. On February 16, in the year 600, Pope Gregory the Great issued a decree from Rome that declared that from that day on, the correct response to a person sneezing would be to say **"God Bless You!"** I'll bet most of us never realized there was a papal decree behind that common saying. I just think that it is really cool to find interesting bits of church trivia like that. A devastating plague was ravaging Rome and a sneeze was thought to be a sign a person had contracted the deadly plague, so a blessing was extremely appropriate and it has lasted down through the centuries to our own time. This Tuesday marks 1410 years that we've been saying **"God Bless You"** when a person sneezes!

The truth of today's First Reading from the Prophet Jeremiah has also withstood the test of time and we can learn that basic truth very readily. **"BLESSED IS THE ONE WHO TRUSTS IN THE LORD, WHOSE HOPE IS THE LORD. HE IS LIKE A TREE PLANTED BESIDE THE WATERS THAT STRETCHES OUT ITS ROOTS TO THE STREAM; IT FEARS NOT THE HEAT WHEN IT COMES, ITS LEAVES STAY GREEN. IN THE YEAR OF DROUGHT, IT SHOWS NO DISTRESS, BUT STILL BEARS FRUIT."**

These words of the Prophet Jeremiah are even older than the words of St. Gregory the Great in authorizing **"God Bless You"** as a reaction to a sneeze. They date back centuries before the time of Christ, and even in our own time their truth is still apparent and still valid.

A tree instinctively sends out its roots towards a source of nourishment, a source of life. Tree roots have been known to even break through roadways and home foundations in their instinctive quest for water and life-giving nourishment. The tree knows if its roots are severed, it will wither and die. It just

keeps persevering even when it meets insurmount-
able obstacles.

We are like the trees of which Jeremiah speaks. We
should be deeply and strongly rooted in Christ. We
should stop at nothing to reach out to Him, to keep
the flow of His life coming into us. Without constant
contact with Christ, our Faith will wither and die.

A tree instinctively seeks water and nourishment.
It's a matter of life and death for the tree. So too,
we Catholic Christians should realize that it is essential for us to draw life from Christ, to send out our
roots to His life-giving water through worshiping
together at Mass each Sunday, through time spent
in sincere prayer, through reading from the words
of the Bible, through receiving the sacraments of
His church, through doing the work of Christ in the
world.

This too is a matter of life and death for us. We all
know people, perhaps we have sometimes even
been people, who ignore God until we need him.
We make a big thing about praying when we are
sick or someone we love is sick or in trouble, but
then as soon as the crisis is over, we go back to just
ignoring God as if we didn't need Him anymore. The
lesson of the tree in today's First Reading is that we
need God all the time, and it is foolish and deadly
to try to make it without Him. No sport, no activity,
no job, no person should ever get between us and
God because God is our only source of everlasting

life. No more than a tree could ever survive without roots could we make it without God. We need to stay connected with Him. It's that simple and it's that important.

So the next time someone sneezes, and you say **"God Bless You"** realize you are sharing in a part of our Catholic history. And the next time you pray, or come to church for Mass, or read the Bible, realize you are sharing in an even more ancient and even more lasting part of our Catholic history. Even more than a tree needs its roots, we need God. There's no getting around that.

As this weekend includes St. Valentine's Day, I thought I would just briefly mention a story I read about a married couple attending a retreat for married couples. Walter and his wife, Anne, listened to the instructor declare: **"It is essential that husbands and wives know the things that are important to each other."** He then addressed the men: **"Can you name your wife's favorite flower"** With that Walter leaned over and gently touched Anne's hand, and whispered in her ear, **"It's Pillsbury All-Purpose, right?"**

A blessing for all married couples. Please stand and hold each other's hand for the blessing.

Blessed are you husbands and wives for the faith you have in God, and for the faith you have in each other. From the first day of your marriage when

God through His priest blessed your lifelong union of minds and hearts and bodies, and continuing through this Valentine's Day weekend, when all in our society celebrate the gift of love, may God continue to bless you and your families with all the strength and grace you need to be living witnesses to God's love for all the world and to God's love for each of you.

First Sunday of Lent - "C"

21 February 2010

FIRST READING: Deuteronomy 26:4-10
PSALM: Psalm 91:1-2, 10-15
SECOND READING: Romans 10:8-13
GOSPEL: Luke 4:1-13

Father Charlie had no sermon in Laughlin for the First Sunday of Lent because Father Michael Moore was preaching the parish mission beginning that weekend. For nearly a decade, Father Michael has been preaching a parish mission here in Laughlin during Lent each year.

Second Sunday of Lent - "C"

28 February 2010

FIRST READING: Genesis 15:5-12, 17-18
PSALM: Psalm 27:1, 7-9, 13-14
SECOND READING: Philippians 3:17-4:1
GOSPEL: Luke 9:28-36

Father Charlie had no sermon in Laughlin for the Second Sunday of Lent because he was in Florida for his brother's 40th birthday celebration that weekend. Yes, sometimes everyone has to leave "Paradise" for awhile.

Kelvin Gordon   Andrew Stanton
Two of My Friends On Fremont Street!

✤ ✤ ✤

Third Sunday of Lent - "C"

7 March 2010

FIRST READING: Exodus 3:1-8, 13-15
PSALM: Psalm 103:1-4, 6-7, 8, 11
SECOND READING: 1 Corinthians 10:1-6, 10-12
GOSPEL: Luke 13:1-9

"Come no nearer! Remove the sandals from your feet, for the place where you stand is holy ground." (Exodus 3:)

I feel like I should reintroduce myself! **Hi...I'm Father Charlie!** I got yelled at by some parishioners and visitors for not preaching the past two weeks so I have to make up for it all today! I'll try not to keep you here too long! But believe me, it's great to be back in Paradise! Father Michael Moore gave a wonderful parish retreat here with over 200 people attending the retreat sessions, and he's very grateful for the $6000 you donated to the St. Patrick's Fathers. Brother Leo DiFiore loved being here last weekend for the mission appeal and you donated over $10,000 to the work of the Passionist Overseas Missions. And our own parish collections have been amazing these past two weeks.....so maybe I should leave town more often! But I have to tell you that I was here on February 14th when we hit a new all-time attendance record for our parish - 2131 people attended Mass that weekend! Now that is awesome!

Well, let me fill you in on the past two weeks in my life.....I was up to Vegas a couple of times for magic shows, ate some incredible meals at a few parishioners' homes - tilapia, broccoli casserole, coleslaw made with olives, baked chicken, cucumber salad, and so much more. Yet somehow 9 pounds has left my body so far in Lent so I must be doing something right. I flew to Florida for 4 days for Michael's 40th birthday, arrived late because of flight delays and even though I had called twice along the way, the hotel cancelled my room reservation! Watched a sideshow performer in Florida walk on broken glass and escape from a straitjacket, went to Downtown Disney (an adult Disney area), and an all-you-can eat pizza buffet at a magic show in Florida. The magician didn't pick me to go on stage, but he did pick a woman from the audience for a card trick. He asked her to choose a card and then place it back in the deck. Then he asked her to tell the audience what card she had picked. She said she had picked the **"TEN OF CLOVERS."** I'm guessing she wasn't much of a card player. I got to sit in one of those new Smart Cars, and ate an ARIPA (sliced corn tortilla filled with cheese and grilled), blessed a new Harley for a parishioner (and negotiated for a ride on it during River Run next month! By the way, that's my fee for motorcycle blessings....one ride around Paradise!) My illegitimate son Eddie got cast in a TV pilot and got a part in Tony and Tina's Wedding up in Las Vegas on the Strip. So now I can say that I'm proud of my son in the Strip show! And I had lunch at an extreme health food café in Florida. An online buddy of mine runs it and we went there for lunch one day. I drank an apple cider vinegar soda and Michael had some mineral-enriched water. Then we ate gluton-free, salt-free, sugar-free, flavor-free bread! My friend, the owner, told Michael about how I had bought some of his mail-order products like healthy muffins and healthy snacks, and then added: **"Charlie is a real cool friend. He doesn't care one bit about health and nutrition, but he still bought my stuff to help me out when I was getting started."** And Michael commented back to him, **"Yeah, you know Charlie well."**

At any rate, that's the short form of what's happened in the last two weeks. Now let's move on!

"Come no nearer! Remove the sandals from your feet, for the place where you stand is holy ground."

In my life, I can only recall four occasions as an adult on which I have been told to take my shoes off. Once when I was on a pilgrimage to Israel and we were about to enter a Mosque, an Islamic place of prayer; a few times when I have visited my friends Joe and Laura. They are both doctors and have a policy in their house that no one is allowed to wear shoes upstairs for fear of bringing germs where their children walk barefoot; every time I visit a state prison and have to go through security to see one of my friends; and in recent years, every time I go through airport security on the way to a flight. Even though I wear basically cheap shoes, they seem to have enough metal in them to set off the detectors. Either that, or I just look threatening!

Being told to take off our shoes reminds us that we are in a different kind of place. Entering a mosque, it is a sign of respect for the religious beliefs of others; going upstairs in Joe and Laura's home, it is a sign of respect for their health concerns for their children; going into a prison, it is a sign of respect for authority and the enforcement of their rules; and going through airport security, it is a reminder that we live in a society in which terrorists unfortunately also exist.

Moses was told to take off his sandals when he approached the burning bush because it was **HOLY GROUND**. He was coming into the presence of Someone who is **INFINITELY HOLY** and Whose presence needs to be respected. Moses was being told to recognize that he was in a place that was different, a place that was special, a place that was holy because God was there. He was not to come into the holy presence of God without being aware of it. This incident in Jewish history is the basis for some of our basic teachings about a church building.

Coming into our little Catholic Church here in Laughlin or even our casino church at the Riverside is also coming into the holy presence of God. That's what we truly believe as Catholics about the **REAL PRESENCE** of Jesus Christ in the tabernacle. That's why a candle always burns in front of the tabernacle. That's why we bless ourselves with holy water as we enter the church, reminding ourselves that we have been baptized and that we are allowed an access to God that is special.

That's also why we genuflect - go down to the floor on our right knee - before we settle into a seat, or go up into the sanctuary. That's why, if it is possible, we kneel during the most sacred part of the Mass when the consecration occurs and Christ becomes present on our altar.

That's why we fast - do without food and drink for at least an hour before receiving Holy Communion. That's why we don't eat or chew gum in church. That's why we turn off our cell phones in church. That's why we don't approach Holy Communion if we are not living according to the teachings of our Catholic Church. God is holy and His Church is holy.

Lent is a good time for all of us to realize just how fortunate we are to be allowed into the Presence of the all-holy God. May we never forget this place is holy, because God is present here in a way that He is not present anywhere else in our lives. Coming to Mass or just coming into the church for a visit should be seen as a standing on holy ground. And we don't even have to take off our shoes to enjoy being here in the presence of God.

God bless you!

Fourth Sunday of Lent - "C"

14 March 2010

FIRST READING: Joshua 5:9, 10-12
PSALM: Psalm 34:2-7
SECOND READING: 2 Corinthians 5:17-21
GOSPEL: Luke 15:1-3, 11-32

The tax collectors and sinners were all gathering to listen to Jesus. They knew He had something important to say, and they knew they should be listening.

I was over in Office Max this week, and one of the salesmen there came up to ask if I needed help finding anything. Actually he said, **"Hey, Boss! Whatcha looking for?"** When I said I was just browsing through the clearance items, he said **"That's cool.... just another day in Paradise!"** Well, that's a line I always use, so it got us started on a conversation. Of course, I had to explain to him that Paradise was actually on the Laughlin side of the river, but we agreed that everyplace in the area was **"close enough to Paradise."** Great conversation, and I got a super deal on a DVD player. Had some awesome homemade macaroni and cheese this week and it was served with cranberry sauce. I never would have thought of that! Of course, I didn't make it. The only homecooked meals I ever have are in other people's homes! I was talking with my brother Michael on the phone and I kept hearing background noise. So I asked him where he was. He said he was making dinner for himself in the kitchen...and then added, **"The kitchen.... you know...that room with a stove."** Hmmm....I think I remember seeing one of those somewhere in the house..... And I was invited to a cornhole tournament this weekend up in Vegas....I had to ask what it was. Apparently there is a group of my friends who gather around a board with a hole cut in the middle of it, and they throw bean bags filled with dried corn at it. If the bag goes in the hole, it scores 5 points. If it lands on the board, it scores 1 point. I decided to just stay down here in Laughlin. And that's pretty much the details of my week.

Speaking of details.....There are so many things in the Gospels that sometimes it is very easy to miss some important details there. For example, in today's Gospel we have the wonderful parable of the Prodigal Son (which Charles Dickins described as **"the greatest short story in the world"**. But even before we get into the parable itself, Luke sets the scene by telling us: **"Tax collectors and sinners were all drawing near to listen to Jesus".** Try to visualize that, these outcasts from society those who had sold out to the Romans by working for them in collecting their taxes, and those known to be sinners, wanted to get near Jesus. They knew He had something important to say to them and they wanted to be near Him to hear it. On the other hand, the so-called self-important people, the Pharisees and the scribes were there complaining against Jesus because He even welcomed the sinners and was not ashamed to eat with them. It is to these two very diverse groups that Jesus addresses the famous parable of the Prodigal Son. I hope we listen to the parable with the same sense of expectation the tax collectors and sinners had. They were far more open to Jesus' message.

The younger son in the story is a really **(REALLY!)** dislikeable character! First of all, he does the unthinkable - he asks his father for his inheritance before his father dies. Parents, imagine one of your children coming to you and saying out loud: **"You know the money I'm going to get from you when you die?.....Well, I want it all now!")** And we think we have family problems! Then, this younger son goes away and wastes the money in a foreign country **"on a life of dissipation"**. Even his reason for coming back home is questionable. He doesn't come back home because he loves his father; he comes back home because he is broke and hungry! He still wants to take from his father. He even rehearses a little speech. It is hard for us to feel any sympathy for him at all. And yet, the father not only takes him back, the father actually has been waiting for his return and runs out to greet him! The father wants him back, he belongs to the family no matter what he has done.

You and I tend to put some obstacles in the way of God's love for us. We sometimes think badly, we act badly, we're not all that loveable sometimes. Those of us who are older might remember a self-help book from the 1960's **"I'M OKAY, YOU'RE OKAY"**. Well sometimes, we're not okay. We're as rude, insensitive, and conniving as that younger son. And yet God pursues us relentlessly. He wants us back even when we don't want Him or don't want Him for the right reasons.

Notice too the father in the parable even wants the elder son back., the one who doesn't understand his generosity. By the way, notice how the elder brother says **"YOUR SON"** to his father, but the father keeps referring to him as **"YOUR BROTHER"**. Even with his seething anger and obvious jealousy, the father wants this son back too.

Most of us have some image of God, some way in which we like to think of Him. May I suggest that this week we try the one from today's Gospel parable?   God is like a loving father, watching the road, looking for His children to come back home where they belong. When we stray from God, isn't it great (wonderful, awesome) to know that He has already planned a party for us when we return? And the slightest turn in his direction that we make will get Him ready setting the table for our welcome back!

Easter is only a few weeks away....and God our Father wants us all home for the holidays.

God bless you!

Fifth Sunday of Lent - "C"

21 March 2010

FIRST READING: Isaiah 43:16-21
PSALM: Psalm 126:1-6
SECOND READING: Philippians 3:8-14
GOSPEL: John 8:1-11

What would Jesus do?

Another awesome week in Paradise, and River Run is only a little more than a month away. Check out Page 7 in today's bulletin for the first announcement of a fun event for us during River Run Week - "The History of the Sideshow!" Just one more thing to make Paradise even more wonderful for us! And speaking of Paradise, one of our parishioners - **Jesse Lewis** - was honored at the Townfest Parade this weekend as Laughlin's Citizen of the Year! Glad to hear that.

I discovered that at age 62, you can buy a **LIFETIME PASS** to all our U.S. National Parks for only $10! What an awesome bargain! Kind of makes getting older worthwhile! And this was a great week for eating.....Had some amazing blackened salmon and baked yams, some homemade Polish pyrogi, and lots of great soda bread and Irish treats on St. Patrick's Day, and some Italian breads and cookies on St. Joseph's Day. And even with all that, our Lenten

Weigh-In Group of 18 people has managed to lose over 51 pounds since Lent began.

Our local parishioners know how proud I am of my illegitimate son, Eddie, and my Jamaican/Puerto Rican brother, Michael. But in case we have some visitors in town, I need to periodically explain that Eddie is not **really** my son, and Michael is not **really** my brother. We're just three guys who are really close friends who feel like family. A few weeks ago, I mentioned Eddie in a sermon and one of the tourists came up to me after Mass and said how much I reminded him of a priest back home in Indiana. I asked **WHY?** And he told me that the priest back in Indiana had been married, and had a son, and became a priest after his wife died. Without thinking it through, I just looked at him and remarked, **"Oh, I've never been married."** Bet he went home with a story on his mind! Eddie's Mom was out visiting this week and she even madecoffee for me and cleaned our kitchen. I told Eddie that his Mom should stay and he should go. She couldn't understand our refrigerator, though. She said that there's nothing in it but Diet Coke, beer, and vegetables. So she went out and bought us peanut butter and bread! We took her to a show up in Vegas. Gave her a choice of seeing **The Rat Pack** (featuring lookalikes of Frank Sinatra, Dean Martin, Joey Bishop and Sammy Davis, Jr.) or a show called **Divas**. She asked her son what **Divas** was. He said it was a group of guys who dress up in women's gowns and sing. She looked at me and said, **"Charlie, can we go see the Rat Pack?"** So we did.

Eddie and I use text-messaging a lot, and that reminded me of how so many people use letters or acronyms in their text messages. An **ACRONYM** is a word formed from the initial letters of a multi-word name. Over the years, there have developed a number of acronyms that have made their way into popular writing and conversation. Most of us know the famous **K.I.S.S.** that is often told to speakers - **KEEP IT SIMPLE, STUPID.** And then there is the one that shows up in tons of emails **L.O.L.** - **LAUGHING OUT LOUD, TTYL - TALK TO YOU LATER** at the end of a message. In fact, one search engine on the Internet lists over 342,000 acronyms in English. Many of my younger friends use acronyms when they send INSTANT MESSAGES. And when I respond using real and complete words, they usually tell me that I write "like an old man!" And there are plenty of religious acronymns too. A few years ago, Mel Gibson's movie **"THE PASSION"** brought an old one to mind - **I.N.R.I.** - the letters seen on most crucifixes which stands for **JESUS OF NAZARETH, KING OF THE JEWS.** One that has made the rounds recently is **P.U.S.H. - PRAY UNTIL SOMETHING HAPPENS.** And then there is the much older one **WWJD. - WHAT WOULD JESUS DO?.**

WWJD - WHAT WOULD JESUS DO? Over the past 15 - 20 years, WWJD has made its way onto bracelets, pins, hats, bumper stickers, tee shirts. But while it is worn by a lot of young people who are not embarrassed by their Christian Faith, this is really not a new question at all. It dates back to a book called **IN HIS STEPS** which was written in 1896 by Charles Sheldon, a pastor in Topeka, Kansas, and it was read one chapter each week to his young adults at Sunday evening Bible Study classes. Remember this was before Television, so this was like coming to a weekly story gradually unfolding. In the book, a NYC pastor proposes to his congregation that they take the Bible seriously. And since they are all sup- posed to be followers of Jesus Christ, he proposes a little Bible experiment - for one year, every time they are faced with an important decision, they should ask themselves the question "What would Jesus do?" before making the decision. The book is fascinating. It chronicles how individual lives were changed and how the whole parish and neighbor- hood were changed just because people actually asked themselves the question "What would Jesus do?" And then acted accordingly.

Of course, I think **WWJD** goes back a whole lot far- ther than 1896. I think it was a question posed by Jesus' original followers. **WHAT WOULD JESUS DO?** led to the formation of the early Christian communities and moral codes. If we are to be true followers of Jesus today, then it should still matter to us that what we do is what Jesus would do if He were in our shoes.

In today's Gospel, the scribes and the Pharisees want to know what Jesus would do when they brought out that woman caught in adultery, but they really weren't prepared for His example when He invited those who had NO sins to go ahead and stone the woman. One by one, they drifted away. Jesus forgave the woman, but He didn't condone her sin of adultery. He even warned her to avoid it in the future.

As Lent is quickly drawing to a close, we might want to keep **WWJD** in mind for the next time we have to face a decision or a situation. Think **WHAT WOULD JESUS DO....** andonly then act accordingly. None of us will go wrong following the Lord's example.

God bless you!

The Indomitable Eddie Ifft!

Palm Sunday

28 March 2010

FIRST READING: Isaiah 50:4-7
PSALM: Psalm22:8-9, 17-20, 23-24
SECOND READING: Philippians 2:6-11
GOSPEL: Luke 22:14-23:56

There is no sermon on Palm Sunday that could ever improve upon the lessons gained by reading the Passion of Our Lord Jesus Christ. This year we read the Passion according to St. Luke.

Easter Sunday

4 April 2010

FIRST READING: Acts 10:34, 37-43
PSALM: Psalm 118:1-2, 16-17, 22-23
SECOND READING: Colossians 3:1-4
GOSPEL: John 20:1-9

Alleluia, the Lord is risen! Alleluia, Alle-luia, Alleluia!

Welcome to Easter in Paradise! For those of you who are from St. John the Baptist here in Laughlin, you already know how happy I am to be here! It's my 36th Easter as a priest, and my 2nd Easter with you here. There is no place else on earth that I would rather be! And I'm thrilled that you're all here to celebrate Easter with me! Faithful parishioners and visitors alike...you are all part of my dream come true to be here in Nevada! It's going to be in the 80's and sunny...New Jersey was never like this!

I love Easter for all the religious reasons, but also for all the goodies it provides. I love the jelly beans and the chocolate! But do you know what the **NUMBER ONE** non-chocolate Easter candy is? It's a marshmallow treat called **PEEPS.** Last Easter more than 700 million Marshmallow Peeps were consumed in the USA. And besides the chicks and bunnies, **PEEPS** also makes stars and hearts and pumpkins and Christmas trees that are so popular that now they are producing over **1.2 BILLION PEEPS** a year. They have been made and sold for over 55 years. And while each **PEEP** has 32 calories, they are a fat-free food! They're one of the very few fat-free foods that actually taste great! So in addition to a lot of chocolate and jelly beans, I have gathered a good supply of **PEEPS** for my post-Easter eating binge!

Every year my Mom would buy me a bunny for Easter, and even though she died 4 years ago, I still keep up the tradition by finding a bunny to add to my collection. Found a particularly good one this year right here in Laughlin. And, of course, I have to show it to you. Yeah, it's really cute. It's not every priest who has a collection of 36 Easter bunnies!

Four years ago, in New Jersey, I celebrated my Mom's funeral Mass. At that time, I received nearly 700 emails/letters/cards and messages from my friends, and thousands of words of comfort spoken to me by people in my parish and surrounding area. Someday I am going to put some of them together in a little booklet because I think they might be helpful for other people who have to face the death of someone they love. One of the most memorable was an encounter with a young student at our parish school. A few weeks after Mom died, he saw me at school and came up to me, grabbed my hand and said, **"Father Charlie, I'm so sorry that your Mom died."** And I was really impressed with his sincerity. Then, still holding my hand, he continued, **"But she's in a better place."** And again I was really impressed that our school had taught this young man such an important truth. But he was still holding my hand so I knew he had more to say. He looked me in the eye and continued to speak saying, **"And you'll be with her soon."** Well, my first thought was **"Maybe not TOO soon! But eventually!"** And then I realized that this young man had learned one of the most important truths of our Catholic Faith - that life never ends! That for those who are faithful, we never lose the ones we love, and someday (maybe not **TOO** soon!), we will be together with them again.

That, by the way, is what we celebrate on Easter - that even death doesn't have the last word. **The last word is not death, but eternal life.** Because Jesus **REALLY DID** rise from the dead on that first Easter Sunday, you and I have incredible hope for our eternal future. And we need that hope. Easter is the pre-eminent celebration of hope and new life! It's a celebration of all the wild possibilities for goodness and happiness that the future holds in store for each and every one of us. It's a yearly reminder of the grace and love with which our God cares for us from birth until we join Him in eternity. Even death cannot limit God's love and grace and care for us. I love Easter! There's something so good about it. I think that even those without a formal religious belief can feel the goodness of Easter. We need that assurance that even death cannot limit God's love and grace and care for us. Maybe that's one of the reasons why churches are so full on Easter Sunday.

Why are you here in church today? Why did you happen to come? Why is it that churches throughout the world are full today, and sadly will be comparatively empty next Sunday? Why are you jamming the pews today?

Perhaps you are here because of **TRADITION. "We always go to church on Easter."** Perhaps you are here today because your mother expects you to sit next to her on Easter and so you are here today. Or maybe you are here today because it's spring... and Easter and spring just go together. It feels like spring...it feels like Easter. Or maybe you are here today because these are tough times for you and for your family, and you and your family are hurting. Maybe you have personally discovered that life is a lot tougher than you thought it was. So you come to receive the strength and grace and power that only Christ can give. Or maybe you are one of those **"Christmas and Easter"** Catholics who actually think this is enough religion for you. You come twice a year for the big holidays. Church is not really your thing. You may have fallen away from the deeper faith you had in childhood. You had it once, but you don't have it anymore. You feel badly about it, but not badly enough to actually do anything about it.

Or maybe you've come here today because you believe. You deeply believe that Jesus conquered sin and death and so you are here to celebrate. Why are you here today? It's something to think about.

You know what I think? I think you are here today because God wants you here today. God wants you to listen to the Scriptures and share in the power and hope of Easter. God brought you here today to hear the Easter message...and to make it part of your life.

It is vitally important that we gather for Easter, that we celebrate together that Christ has risen from the dead. Easter reminds us each year that death is not the end, that there is a whole lot more to life than what we can see and experience during our relatively few years here on earth. If it were not for the Resurrection of Jesus, you and I might be tempted to just give up when things get rough, or when loved ones get sick or die. We might mistakenly think life is only what we can see or touch. We might fail to realize that life, real life, is a whole lot more.

People knew that Jesus had risen from the dead because they saw the results of the Resurrection in the lives of Jesus' followers. It was their lives that made the Resurrection so convincing. This Easter I would like to suggest it is truly **OUR LIVES** which continue to make the Resurrection so convincing. It we do not live as people who believe in the Resurrection, then there really is no other way for people to see it's truth in our world today. We are very important to God in spreading His message of hope.

Sure there will be obstacles, but we have the strength and power of God behind us when we choose to do what is right and good, even when it is difficult or unpopular. God brought you here today to strengthen your Faith, to give you hope, to ease your sorrows, to share His own life with you. When I wish you a HAPPY EASTER, believe me it is not just chocolate and jelly beans and PEEPS and spring flowers I want you to have! I want you to have to joy of Easter, the power of Easter, the faith and hope and strength of Easter. May God bless you for being here today. This is where God wants you to be!

Happy Easter to all of you as we celebrate Jesus' Resurrection. And thank you for being where God wants you to be.

God bless you!

2nd Sunday of Easter - Divine Mercy Sunday - "C"

11 April 2010

FIRST READING: Acts 5:12-16
PSALM: Psalm 118:2-4, 13-15, 22-24
SECOND READING: Revelation 1:9-13, 17-19
GOSPEL: John: 20:19-31

We have so much for which to be thankful. God is so merciful to us!

What an incredible Easter here in Paradise! We have nearly 2050 people join us for the Easter Masses (an increase of 200 people over last year!), and our Easter collection is nearly $13,000 (an increase of nearly $1000 over last year!), 9 candidates in our RCIA program completed their sacraments of initiation at the Easter Vigil (more than double last year's number!), and I got to administer the Sacrament of Confirmation to them (that's the closest I will ever get to being a bishop!). I got four beautiful stuffed bunnies and a ton of **PEEPS** to eat, along with salmon patties, deviled eggs, garlic mashed potatoes,tomato soup, and an awesome carrot cake! And on Easter Sunday I got treated to an incredible seafood brunch after the Masses so I was stuffed with crab and shrimp and scallops (among many other things). We are all so blessed to be living here or visiting here in Paradise! And we have so much for which to be thankful!

And I've had an awesome Easter Week! Eddie got comp tickets to see the **VIVA ELVIS** show at the ARIA in CityCenter up in Vegas. He was going to see it with a friend, but his friend bailed out at the last minute so I get a call on Monday night at 7PM asking **"Hey Dad, watcha doing tonight? Want to come and see the Elvis show?"** After I said, **"Oh, yeah, right, I'm 2nd choice"**, I got in the car and drove to Vegas for the 9:30 PM show. On Tuesday, I got to see Eddie in **TONY AND TINA'S WEDDING** up in Vegas. For fun, I wore one of his bright pink-striped ties, so all night long I was nicknamed **"Hey, Pink Tie!"**. I got even with him on Wednesday, by taking a friend to lunch at the restaurant where Eddie works and having him wait on us. I kept sending him back for things like catsup, more iced tea, extra napkins....ah, it's sweet to pick on him! Was having so much fun that I got very little sleep..... going to bed at 5:35 AM is fun, but a little hard on me! Oh, and I played $20 in a slot machine up in Vegas, and walked away with $414.00 from it! Can buy a lot of **PEEPS** with that!

And Friday back in Laughlin was awesome too! Unexpectedly I got paid back $80 that I had lent out a few months ago, and got a call that a side-show buddy Tim Cridland (who performs under the stage name TORTURE KING) was passing through town so we meet up late Friday night for a few hours to share show biz news. And I got invited to watch a friend get a huge tattoo on his back on Saturday. I'd probably never get a tattoo myself (I don't like needles), but I love seeing the incredible artwork on someone else. And I got to bless my very first tattoo....so if you ever need one blessed, I now know how to do it! So my Easter Week has been AWESOME! I hope yours has been too!

There are many names for the Sunday after Easter. At various times and in various places, it has been called **LOW SUNDAY** (because of the drop in atten- dance compared with Easter); **SUNDAY IN WHITE** (because the newly-baptized used to wear their white garments to Mass for the Sunday following Easter); **DIVINE MERCY SUNDAY** (in honor of the cel- ebration of Jesus' unlimited mercy to all of us.) But my personal favorite has always been a medieval tradition of calling this Sunday **BRIGHT SUNDAY,** a day on which we renew our **EASTER JOY**. We, as faithful Catholic Christians, can laugh in triumph over the devil. In the big picture, he's just a **COSMIC LOSER** in the battle for our souls! We can **LAUGH** at him because **JESUS** is the **ULTIMATE WINNER**. And you and I are associated with Jesus' victory over sin and death because of our baptism.

During a speech to priests about preaching, Bishop Robert Morneau (Auxiliary bishop of Green Bay, Wisconsin) said: **"If you can make your people smile even a little bit on a Sunday when they come to Mass, do it. They've had a hard week and it is**

good for them to laugh in church."I try to follow that advice whenever possible.

Many of us who come to church faithfully no doubt bring worries and cares with us. And we can't just check them at the door, or turn them off like we do our cell phones before entering here. Certainly we are concerned with the Middle East, and the safety of our American Forces overseas, particularly in Iraq and Afghanistan. Certainly we're concerned with terrorist activities. Certainly we're concerned with situations within our own families of divorce, death or sickness of a spouse or parent or child, bread-winners being out of work, and so many other situations in life. We have to hold on to the belief that God is still in charge. And while we might feel there is very little we can do as individuals in these various crises, we can most certainly pray that God will shed His light and give to us and to those in authority the wisdom they need to deal with these situations. And we can also pray that those whose lives have been affected might find the peace and healing only Jesus can provide. These situations may certainly TEST our Faith, but they should never be allowed to weaken it or destroy it. Like Thomas, in today's Gospel, we need the re-assurance of Jesus. And Jesus re-assures us too. He invites our belief. He does not force us to believe. And even when we fail, God's mercy is boundless and unde-servedly generous. You'll see in the bulletin that today we celebrate Divine Mercy Sunday, so I'd like to share my favorite story about God's mercy:

GOD'S MERCY: A man dies and goes to heaven. Of course, St. Peter meets him at the Pearly Gates. St. Peter says, "Here's how it works. You need 100 points to make it into heaven. You tell me all the good things you've done, and I give you a certain number of points for each item, depending on how good it was. When you reach 100 points, you get in." "Okay," the man says, "I was married to the same woman for 50 years and never cheated on her, even in my heart." "That's wonderful," says St. Peter, "that's worth three points!" "Three points?" he says. "Well, I attended church all my life and supported its ministry with my tithes and service." "Terrific!" says St. Peter. "That's certainly worth a point." "One point!?""I started a soup kitchen in my city and worked in a shelter for homeless veterans." "Fantastic, that's good for two more points," he says. "Two points!?!!"

Exasperated, the man cries. "At this rate, the only way I'll get into heaven is by the grace and mercy of God." "Bingo, 100 points!" says St. Peter. "Now you understand! Come on in!"

We all need God's mercy. Think of how merciful God has been to you....and then try to imitate God's mercy with each other. Now that's how to celebrate Divine Mercy Sunday!

God bless you!

Oh, What a Night!

(With Jason, Michael and Thom!)

3rd Sunday of Easter - "C"

18 April 2010

FIRST READING: Acts 5:27-32, 40-41
PSALM: Psalm 30:2-4, 5-6, 11-13
SECOND READING: Revelation 5:11-14
GOSPEL: John 24:1-19

God really does know EVERYTHING!

Another amazing week in Paradise! Homemade Polish pirogi, pasta with white clam sauce, and an incredible cheesecake/carrot cake combination. And I even found a post-Easter sale on **PEEPS**....only $.18 a package....now I'm stocked up for the year! And I got my income taxes mailed in on April 15th.... never can seem to do that early, but I managed to make it on time. And River Run is this coming week! I love River Run! So you know where I'm going to be in my free time! I've even lined up a few rides with the bikers already! And life with Eddie continues to be an education in parenting....at 26, he's going to drive me insane! This week, he claimed he had a broken rib because he had a terrible pain in his ribcage. While we were talking, I looked at his bed and noticed that he had been sleeping on his wireless computer keyboard! I suggested that perhaps removing the keyboard before going to sleep would alleviate the pain! And he forgot his grunge jeans and flannel shirt when we were meeting for a show, so I had to bring them and let him change in the backseat of my car. We use the same cologne so I thoughtfully brought along my bottle of it in case he needed it. He drenched himself in it. I said, **"But you never use that much cologne!"** And he said, **"Yeah, but it's okay, this bottle is yours."** But the best thing was when I noticed that for the past two weeks we have to get up and turn the TV on without using a remote. When I asked what happened to the remote, he explained that he had fallen asleep with it on one of the couches, and he thinks it's somewhere inside or under one of the couches. But he didn't feel like looking for it. I walked over to him, cupped his face in my hands, looked him in the eyes, and said, **"Is there anyone in there?!"** I'm beginning to understand what parents of teens and young adults go through. **I don't know everything yet, but I'm learning more every day.**

In today's Gospel according to St. John, Jesus asks Peter three times: **"DO YOU LOVE ME?"** And three times, Peter answers: **"YES, LORD."** Peter really does mean it, but by the third time Jesus asks the question, Peter is hurt by the repetition of the question, and so he adds a bit to his response: **"LORD, YOU KNOW EVERYTHING. YOU KNOW THAT I LOVE YOU!"**

Did you know that three-fourths of all the eggplant used in the world comes from New Jersey? **Did you know that you burn more calories sleeping that you do watching television?** Did you know that American Airlines saved $40,000 in 1987 by eliminating one olive from each salad served in First Class? **Did you know that Walt Disney was afraid of mice?** Did you know that apples, not caffeine, are more efficient at waking you up in the morning? **Did you know that donkeys kill more people annually than plane crashes?** Did you know that no piece of paper can be folded in half more than 7 times? **Did you know that Tom Clancy, the author, is afraid of flying?**

Well, those are just a few things you would have to know if you actually were to know **EVERYTHING!** And that's the amazing thing about God. **He really does know everything!** He knows everything that ever was, is, or will be. He knows all the details about how things work and why things happen.

It is truly a **FRIGHTENING** and yet I think **WONDERFULLYCOMFORTING** thought that God does indeed know everything. This means we can't put one over on God, we can't hide our true feelings from Him. We can't deceive Him with a lie, or a concealed word or action. **He knows everything.** This can be truly frightening. I'm still amazed at the number of people who would actually lie to a priest, like those who want me to sign of sponsor certificate for them and who tell me that they really do come to church almost every week. They just go to the 11:00 A.M. Mass here or they go to the Mass that the **"other priest"** always celebrates. Sometimes I catch them in their lies, sometimes I just pity them. I wonder if they actually think that because they try to put one over on me, they can deceive God and get away with it. This can be really **FRIGHTENING**.

But the fact that God really does know **EVERY- THING** is also a **WONDERFULLY COMFORTING** thought. It means that even when horrible trage- dies occur, God knows and understands the pain we're going through. It means He will always know just how sincere our intentions are. It means when we suffer some injury or pain or grief, God will know exactly what we are going through even if no one else understands. **It means that He can read our thoughts and know when we are really trying, even when we don't always succeed.** For me, and prob- ably for you, this is wonderfully comforting.

Today would be a good day to think a bit about God's complete knowledge of each one of us. Peter could stand before the Lord, and even with all his faults and failings, say **"LORD, YOU KNOW EVERYTHING. YOU KNOW THAT I LOVE YOU!"**

Hopefully, you and I can say the same thing to the Lord today and every day of our lives. Maybe we should try it together: **"LORD, YOU KNOW EVERY- THING. YOU KNOW THAT I LOVE YOU!"**

God bless you!

4th Sunday of Easter - "C"

25 April 2010

FIRST READING: Acts 13:14, 43-52
PSALM: Psalm 100:1-3, 5
SECOND READING: Revelation 7: 9, 14-17
GOSPEL: John 10: 27-30

Yes, we are like sheep, and the Lord is really our Shepherd.

It's **RIVER RUN** here in Paradise! What an awesome week! I love **RIVER RUN!** Oh, I wouldn't like Laughlin to be this crowded and noisy **EVERY** week, but one week a year like this just makes Paradise even better! I got out for a ride on a Trike (Honda Goldwing) and even got my very own Do-rag. Not sure if it was the do-rag on my head or the Evil Clowns Tee shirt I was wearing, but I met some parishioners along the way and had to reintroduce myself! Got to see the American Hellriders**(Corey, Mike and Logan)** race their speed bikes inside a huge silo... noisy, but incredible skill! Was talking to a couple of them after the show, and they were telling me how much they liked coming to Laughlin! See, even hellriders think this is Paradise! And our History of the Sideshow event at the Pioneer on Tuesday night brought out over 130 people, and we raised just about $1000 for the Colorado River Food Bank! And at the auction that night I won the actual **BED OF NAILS!** So now I own an authentic sideshow prop! It's being used in the shows this week by the sideshow freaks, Ses Carny and Professor Chumley, and then it will be in my office. I'm thinking it might make an interesting penance for folks who come in for confession....**"You get 5 minutes on the bed of nails!"** One of my friends commented, **"What kind of sheets do you use on a bed of nails?"** And I responded, **"Holey ones, or they soon will be!"** I've been at Ses' show each night. Their language could use some cleaning up, but their sideshow skills are awesome!

The most interesting part of my week was spending Monday afternoon with these two sideshow freaks, Ses and Chumley. We went to lunch at Black Bear. I told them I was paying,Ses said he would not allow that. So after the meal, the waiter brought the check and put it in the middle of the table, Ses and I reached for it, but he knocked over a bottle of vinegar and I grabbed the check and stuffed it into my shirt pocket. He told me to hand it over, or else. I said **"NO"**. A few minutes later, he got up to find the men's room, walked behind me, and put me in a headlock while shoving his hand into my shirt pocket to grab the check! Somehow I remembered an old piece of self-defense advice, and grabbed his wrist, shoving my two thumbs into the nerves on the inside of the wrist. He screamed, **"You can't do that, you're a priest!"** After our tussle, I'm not sure we're allowed back in the Black Bear anymore! Unfortunately, he eventually got to the cashier, had them pull up a duplicate on the cash register, and paid the bill. He came back to me and told me I could keep the worthless piece of paper in my shirt pocket. But I did get even.... at the show each night, audience members have the opportunity to come up and staple money on him as part of the sideshow.....so, of course, I got in line, and stapled a $5 on his chest while staring him in the eye and saying, **"I win! You have to keep it now."** What an awesome week! I know there are some people who are not fond of River Run, but I think it's all in how you see it. Yeah, it's different, and loud, but it's also exciting and beautiful! Depends on how you look at it and how you see it.....

Speaking of seeing.....three years ago this week, I had cataract surgery.The results were **IMMEDIATE** and **AWESOME**! For the first time in years, I could see faces in the back of the church! I was like a kid with a new toy! **Did you know that there are numbers on the little buttons of the microwave?** Man, that made timing what I'm cooking so much easier! And apparently that week they started printing newspapers and restaurant menus so much darker! **And did you know that on almost every street corner there is a little sign that has the street name on it?** Wow, that made it so much easier to find addresses! Of course, there were some drawbacks. One of the first people I met after the surgery was a woman I know from the parish. She asked how the surgery had gone and had my sight improved a lot. I looked at her and said, **"Wow, you've got gray roots!"** (Probably not the most tactful thing to say!) And my friend Joey, who knew how much I loved Las Vegas emailed me to tell me: "Gee, now you're going to find out that all these years you've been going to **Sin City**, not **Vatican City**!" At any rate, I'm thrilled with my new ability to see and my sight has remained really good...so those of you in the back of the church had better behave.....I can still see you!

Speaking of seeing, how do you see God? How would you describe Him? What is He like? In the Bible, God is described in many ways. He is the LIGHT OF THE WORLD, a JUDGE, a KING, a TEACHER, our CREATOR, a ROCK, a SAVIOR, a FRIEND and so many more. In the Book of Psalms, He is described as a **SHEPHERD**..."The Lord is my Shepherd, there is nothing I shall want." And Jesus picks up on that image in today's very brief Gospel passage **"My sheep hear my voice. I know them, and they follow Me."**

Just a few thoughts on shepherds and sheep.....If God is our shepherd, then we are like sheep, and like sheep we need a Good Shepherd to GUIDE us, to PROTECT us, and to HELP us.

Because of their wooly coats, sheep can become tangled in brambles when they don't watch where they're going. The more they struggle the free themselves, the more tangled they become. They need the Shepherd to come over and rescue them. And sheep aren't very good about finding food and water, they need the Shepherd to lead them where they will be fed.

Sometimes sheep fall over and can't get back on their feet. They need the Shepherd to help them up. Sometimes sheep wander off from the flock, they need the Shepherd to come looking for them and bring them back.

Sheep can't protect themselves very well. They don't have sharp claws or sharp teeth, and they don't run very fast. They need the Shepherd to protect them from harm.

Like sheep, we need a Shepherd. We need Jesus. Sometimes that's hard to admit....kind of like admitting that we need to do something about our poor eyesight. But when we do admit it, when we do make an attempt to follow Jesus the Good Shepherd, a whole new world opens up for us. It's a world in which we're guided, protected and helped in so many ways that it's almost impossible to describe them to someone who hasn't experienced it, or hasn't even noticed it.

Today, think of God as the Good Shepherd, the One who wants to guide, protect and help you. See if you can't clear out the eyes of your soul so that you can see how much you need Him in your life. And then, do you best to follow wherever He is leading you. It's like a whole new world out there for those who are able to see, and willing to follow. And it's even more exciting than River Run in Paradise!

God bless you!

Ben Stone and I after His Show!

5th Sunday of Easter - "C"

2 May 2010

FIRST READING: Acts 14:21-27
PSALM: Psalm 145:8-13
SECOND READING: Revelation 21:1-5
GOSPEL: John 13:31-35

GOOD will eventually conquer EVIL, GOOD is always stronger and longer-lasting than evil, there are more GOOD people than BAD people in the world.

Some great times in Paradise this week.....Our locals know that I won an authentic bed-of-nails at River Run last week, so I have it at home. I had hired someone to do some yard work for me and I invited him in to the house for something to drink while I wrote out the check to pay him. I forgot that I had the bed of nails on the floor. You should have seen his face when he came into the house and saw it! The look on his face said, **"What have I gotten myself into?!"**

But the best part of my week was Thursday night. Frank and Elna, a couple I had met on their honeymoon back in 1970 - **40 years ago** - surprised me here in Laughlin. We have only seen each other once in those 40 years! Actually I enjoyed their honeymoon. We were on a cruise on the Queen Elizabeth II, and Frank got sick the first night when the ship started to move, so I got to dance with his wife more on the first night of their honeymoon than he did! We went out to dinner here in Paradise on Thursday, and compared 40 year old pictures, and decided we hadn't changed all that much other than me dying my hair white so I'd look older! Reunions are awesome fun!

And this weekend begins the month of May, a month traditionally dedicated to Mary, Our Blessed Mother. I remember a story I once heard about a **nervous young priest** who was a really awful preacher. An older priest offered to help him. He told him that you need to tell stories that catch people's attention, and that will make preaching easier. The young priest asked him for an example, so the old priest said, "Suppose you want to talk about Mary, Our Blessed Mother. You start out by saying **I'VE GOT A SECRET**.....and everyone likes to hear a secret so they will listen to you. Then you continue with **I'VE GOT A GIRLFRIEND**....and that will really get them listening to you. And then you tell them, **AND HER NAME IS MARY**.....and you go on into your sermon about the Blessed Mother with everyone listening."

Well the very next weekend, the nervous young priest decides to try it. He goes to the pulpit and starts with **I'VE GOT A SECRET!** And, sure enough, everyone listens intently. And then he continues, **THE PASTOR HAS A GIRLFRIEND**......and **I CAN'T REMEMBER HER NAME!** Good, now that you're all listening......

Today at the 8AM Mass, we celebrated First Holy Communion with 11 of our parish children. Hope Castillo has done a wonderful job of preparing them for this milestone in their religious development, and I'm thrilled as a priest to see them come forward to receive Jesus for the very first time.

Of course, I thought back to my own First Holy Communion in May of 1955 - 55 years ago. I received my First Holy Communion before the parents of our First Communicants were even born! For my First Holy Communion, I was dressed in a pure white suit and white shirt and tie. I looked like a cheap imitation of John Travolta in **"Saturday Night Fever!"** I remember going to the Lyndhurst Diner with my parents and spilling an entire glass of fresh orange juice down the front of my white suit. Could never get that stain out!

I'm sure if you think about it, you can recall your own First Holy Communion Day. It had to feel special to receive Jesus for the very first time in your life whether it was in a big cathedral or even in a small country church.

One of the things I do for our First Communicants is to give each of them a little sign to post on the refrigerator. **(MASS SCHEDULE)** As you can see, I am not at all subtle about it! **Catholics go to Mass each Sunday**. It's just what we do! I know parents like to have my helpful reminder.

Today's readings remind us of some things that are as plain and simple as my little sign, they are just what we do as Catholics. We try to follow Jesus' command: **"Love one another"** even when that is difficult to do. And we try to believe some really basic things about life in this world: **GOOD will eventually conquer EVIL, GOOD is always stronger and longer-lasting than evil, there are more GOOD people than BAD people in the world.** That's good for our First Communicants to know, and it's good for us to know too!

While I'm on the topic of Communion, it might be good to make a reminder to those who do come faithfully about how to receive Communion. We make a slight bow of our head as we approach for Communion. Then, if you are receiving the host on your tongue, you need to come forward and **ACTUALLY OPEN YOUR MOUTH** with your tongue out. I'm not going to reach in there! If you're going to receive Communion on your hand, then you need to hold your hands out, **ONE OVER THE OTHER,** and form a flat surface for me to place the host on. Not a bowl, not crossed fingers, and not GRABBING the host out of my hand. As one ancient saint put it, **YOU ARE FORMING A THRONE ON WHICH THE KING OF THE UNIVERSE WILL BE PLACED.** And, of course, things like gum and candy should never be in your mouth in church anyway, so you can say **AMEN** clearly when I say **THE BODY OF CHRIST.**

So today, as we come up for our Communion, whether it is our second or our 12,000th, breathe a prayer of gratitude to God for loving us so much. And pray for your own parents and teachers who have helped you to remain faithful along the way. And to anyone who has ever taught you to show love and to believe in the power of goodness.

We have something that no one else in the world has access to in the same way. Only those who are faithfully living our Catholic Faith are allowed to receive Jesus in Communion. In time, this is what usually leads people to come back to regular worship, or to get their marriages validated in the church, or to go to confession if they have been missing Mass. They miss Communion so much that they have strength to do something about it.

Communion is a great gift and privilege for those who are trying to be faithful. God loves us so much that He actually chooses to come to us in this special way. It should make every Sunday a special day in our lives as we come here together to receive the Lord Jesus Christ.

First Holy Communion Day is a real blessing for those receiving Jesus for the very first time, and for our whole community. It reminds us just how blessed we are to have God so close to us.

God bless you!

6th Sunday of Easter - "C"

9 May 2010

FIRST READING: Acts 15:1-2, 22-29
PSALM: Psalm 67:2-3, 5, 6, 8
SECOND READING: Revelation 21:10-14, 22-23
GOSPEL: John 14:23-29

The best years of my life were spent in the arms of another man's wife.....my mother!

Another great week in Paradise! Eddie and I actually tried out the bed of nails that I won in the River Run auction a few weeks ago. The first thing we discovered was that it's not good to lay on a bed of nails with your head on the nails. Man, that hurts! But we had fun, took some pics, and decided to keep our regular jobs instead of running off to join a sideshow. Next year at River Run, I'm going to try to learn another sideshow skill - maybe fire-breathing! Now that would be useful for a fire-and-brimstone type sermon!

With today being Mother's Day, I've had a few people comment on how hard it must be for me today remembering my Mom who died four years ago. While I really appreciate their concern, Mother's Day has never been a sad day for me. Mom and I had wonderful times together. And there is nothing I can look back on and say, **"Oh, I wish we**

would have done this, or I wish we would have gone there." We did all of it, and those memories just get better with each passing year. If there's anything I wish for the children (and adults) in our congregation today, it's that they might enjoy their Moms as much as I enjoyed mine. My Mom used to like to tell her friends about a time on our back porch when I was about 8 with a group of friends and Mom was listening in from the kitchen window. My friends were all bragging about their Mom's and the jobs they had or the education they had. My Mom at the time didn't go out to work and didn't have more than a high school diploma. So when my turn came, all I said was **"My Mom is older than your Mom's!"** That worked with my friends, but for some reason Mom wasn't looking too happy when I went back into the house!

Take the time to tell your Mom that you love her, and be sure to take the time to pray for your Mom today. To all our mothers in the congregation, I wish you the very best of days today! There's a wonderful old saying, I believe from Spain, which states: **"An ounce of mother is worth a pound of clergy!"** Thanks for making my job easier because of all you do!

Mother's Day is a part of our history. For nearly **100** years, we have been celebrating the 2nd Sunday of May as Mother's Day. I found a little story that might be appropriate to pass along today.

A teacher was trying to teach her class about fractions. After the lesson, she tested one of the boys who was from a large family. "Johnny," she said, "There are 6 people in your family. You Mom bakes a pie, and she cuts it up for you. What percentage of the pie will you receive?" Johnny thought for a minute, and then said "I'll get ONE-FIFTH of the pie." The teacher said, "Now, remember there are SIX people in your family. How big would your piece of the pie be?" And again, Johnny said, "ONE-FIFTH". The teacher said, "No, Johnny, you don't understand fractions!" And Johnny said respectfully, "No, teacher, you don't understand my Mom. She would have said that she didn't want any pie."

To all our Mom's and to all who have been like mothers to us, today is your day! God bless you for all you have done and continue to do for us. You're in our prayers and thoughts today.

HISTORY! Sometimes when you mention a subject like history, people immediately turn you off because they think whatever you're about to say will be boring. I never really liked history when I was in school. In fact, I used to routinely fall asleep in my college American history classes. My classmates used to take bets about how many minutes I would make it into the after-lunch American history class before I nodded off! But there are three segments of history that I do like. I like **ANCIENT HISTORY** (the Egyptians, the Greeks and the Romans);

I like **MILITARY HISTORY.** I was astounded to learn in one of my military history courses about a Chinese General named SUN LEE who lived in the 8th century before Christ (nearly 3000 years ago). He is the man credited with having discovered one of the most basic laws of military strategy. He discovered the fact that it is usually better to attack downhill than uphill! (I would have thought that something like that would be self-evident!) And the third type of history I like is **CHURCH HISTORY** - where we came from and what happened in our past as a church. I just want to say a few words about **CHURCH HISTORY** today. Please try not to imitate me in my college days. Don't fall asleep on me!

Today's first reading from the **ACTS OF THE APOSTLES** tells about a pivotal event in the history of the Catholic Church. It is set in approximately the year 50 A.D. - some 17 years after Jesus had died on the cross and the rose from the dead. In those 17 years, even without the Internet, TV, computers, and modern communications, the Catholic Church had grown and developed throughout the Mediterranean world. Thousands of people had been converted, but almost all of them were Jewish. After all, Jesus was Jewish and all the Apostles were Jewish. The Roman authorities, in fact, thought of the Christians as merely a group within Judaism. And that was just the way things were. The early Christians used to worship in the synagogue on the Sabbath (Saturday) and then gather for the Eucharist on Sunday with those who believed in Jesus. There were no church buildings, so they used to meet in one another's homes. They even thought of themselves as practicing Jews.

Less than two decades after Jesus' death and resurrection, Greeks and Romans and other pagans began to express an interest in Christianity, but many Christians felt that the only way to become a Christian was to first become a good, practicing Jew. This meant observing all the Jewish laws and rituals; it meant circumcision for the males; it meant keeping the Jewish feasts, etc. For pagans, who had no interest whatsoever in Judaism, this was not an attraction. For the Christians, it posed a real dilemma - **EXACTLY WHAT MADE A PERSON A CHRISTIAN?   WAS BAPTISM JUST RESTRICTED TO THE JEWS?**

The decision could have gone either way. And, in fact, it was probably much more likely to have gone in favor of the Gentiles having to submit to Judaism. Had that happened, the Catholic Church would have probably spread only within the Jewish territories. And some 20 years later, when Rome stepped in and destroyed the Temple in Jerusalem and drove the Jews out of Israel, the Christians would have been decimated and not have survived much at all. But what happened in the year 50, at what is called the **FIRST COUNCIL** of the Church, was a decision to admit anyone to Christianity merely on the basis of BAPTISM. You didn't have to become Jewish to become Christian! **"IT IS**

THE DECISION OF THE HOLY SPIRIT, AND OURS TOO, NOT TO LAY ON YOU ANY BURDEN BEYOND THAT WHICH IS STRICTLY NECESSARY." The decision we read about in today's First Reading opened the Catholic Church to the world! Were it not for that decision, all those of us who are not Jewish in family background would probably never have come from Catholic Christian families. We'd probably be practicing pagans today, outside worshiping a tree or something!

Just a little bit of Church History..... but I thought you should know how very important that decision was so many years ago. We should be very grateful that it opened up the Catholic Church to our ancestors and to us. It might even make us think a little about the far-reaching effects of the decisions we make. Sometimes even what seems to be a minor decision might have very long-lasting consequences. We should always think before we act.....and like the Apostles, we should pray too.

There is another reason for mentioning history today. We are living in some very troubling times. We have seen evils done in our lifetime by terrorists that rank among the most despicable acts in the history of the world. We have seen political corruption on a grand scale. We have seen economic chaos. We have seen people who claim to be Catholic, yet refusing to live by the teachings of the Catholic Church. All of this could lead us to fear that the end must be near, that God just cannot tolerate any more. And yet, with all this, the clear lesson of history is that Jesus did not promise us that there would be no serious problems. He promised He would remain with us and He told us he would send the Holy Spirit to teach us and dwell with us. We need to remember His saying in today's Gospel: **"DO NOT LET YOUR HEARTS BE TROUBLED OR AFRAID."** The Church has endured a lot in these past 2000 years, and it has survived, and it will continue to survive. The lesson of history is that God is still working His purposes even in the darkest times. We need to hold on to that promise today especially. And we should always think before we act.....and like the Apostles, we need to pray continuously for the strength and wisdom we so desperately need to confront the challenges and problems of our time in history. God will not leave us without His guidance if we sincerely seek it. That is the real lesson of history for us as Catholic Christians. God is always near us. We can always go to God. I guess it's likely this is a lesson our Moms taught us.

God bless you!

Worth 1000 Words!

The Ascension of the Lord

16 May 2010

FIRST READING: Acts 1:1-11
PSALM: Psalm 47:2-3, 6-7, 8-9
SECOND READING: Ephesians 1:17-23
GOSPEL: Luke 24:46-53

There is no backup plan!

Another amazing week in Paradise! And this weekend we hit more than 100 degrees officially for the first time in 2010, so summer can't be far behind. And I found a new reason to enjoy my cell phone. Eddie had a really hot date this week..... model quality.....so he texted me throughout the date to keep me posted. **"Going well!"..."Going really well!"..."Going amazingly well!"** When I saw him, I asked if the girl knew he was texting a priest throughout their date, and he said No, he would just do it when she wasn't looking. **So girls, when you go out on dates, just remember that the guy could be texting details of it to a priest!**

I picked up two hitchhikers on my way from Laughlin to Vegas last week. They were probably in their mid-20's, professional hippies, and trying to get to Oklahoma. Joe was abandoned by his parents when he was just 13 and has lived on his own since then. Roy was just wandering around trying to make a living. They fixed cars, played guitar and a digeridoo, to make some money.We had a great conversation on the trip. I now know there's a red light on the last car of a freight train. If it's not lit, then you shouldn't try to jump on the train because it may be weeks before it leaves. If it's lit, then the train will leave within 12 hours. If it's blinking, then the train leaves within 4 hours. And you should never try to jump onto a freight train unless you can count the lug nuts on the moving wheels.....otherwise the train is going too fast. And when you jump off one, just leave your backpack on and curl up into the fetal position and roll off...that way you won't get hurt too bad. The most beautiful story they told me was that up in Vegas they had no money so they joined some slot clubs and tried to use the free play. They were able to make $30.00 between them. But when they came out of the casino, they saw some homeless old men (you know, Joe said, like your age!) and they figured someday that might be them so they split the $30 with the men. By the time I picked them up, they had $6.00 between them and they wanted to give it to me to thank me for giving them a ride to Vegas. I had some extra money so I shared it with them and told them to call me the next time they were passing through the area. Love meeting new people. And I know many people say it is not safe to pick up hitchhikers, but people who know me, know that I do it.

People who know me know that I collect OWLS. I've done it since I was in high school. At one point, I had over 2000 owls! I was at a meeting once in San

Antonio, Texas, and a group of my friends who are Baptist ministers took me out for dinner one night. They said they had found the perfect place for us to eat and that I would love it! Well, we walked past a few country music bars (I love country music!), but we didn't go into any of them. And we walked past some Italian restaurants, but we didn't go into them. Finally, we went into this one place and I was really surprised. Remember, the group I was with were all Baptist ministers, who didn't drink alcohol. And the place they brought me to that night was HOOTERS. The one and only time I have eaten in a HOOTERS was with a group of Baptist ministers! They told me they were so happy because they had found an entire restaurant devoted to OWLS! **Boy, were they surprised!**

Have you ever heard of something called the GREAT COMMISSION? It's a very popular expression in Protestant theology, and is contained in today's first reading where Jesus says, **"You will receive power when the Holy Spirit comes upon you, and you will be my witnesses in Jerusalem, throughout Judea and Samaria, and to the ends of the earth."**

A really good friend of mine, who happens to be one of the Baptist ministers who took me to HOOT-ERS, once preached an hour-long sermon on the GREAT COMMISSION. He told me that his Baptist congregation would feel cheated if he didn't preach for at least an hour! I told him that a Catholic congregation would have a different view of a sermon that long! I promise I won't preach an hour-long sermon to you today. But I do want to remind you of what the GREAT COMMISSION is.

It is Jesus' final instructions to His Apostles and disciples, just before He ascended into heaven. St. Matthew's Gospel spells it out even more clearly than today's first reading which gives us a part of it:

Jesus said to them: **"All power in heaven and on earth has been given to Me. Go, therefore, and make disciples of all nations, baptizing them in the name of the Father and of the Son and of the Holy Spirit, teaching them to observe all that I have commanded you. And, behold, I am with you always, until the end of the age."** The GREAT COMMISSION is to take what we have learned from Jesus and to share it with the world around us.

There's a great old story about how Jesus after his ascension into Heaven, was surrounded by the Holy Angels who began to enquire about his work on earth. Jesus told them about His birth, life, preaching, death and resurrection, and how He had accomplished the salvation of the world. The angel Gabriel asked, "Well, now that You are back in Heaven, who will continue Your work on earth?" Jesus said, **"While I was on earth, I gathered a group of people around me who believed in me and loved me. They will continue to spread the Gospel and carry on the work of the Church."** Gabriel was perplexed. **"You mean Peter, who**

denied you three times and all the rest who ran away when You were arrested? You mean to tell us that You left them to carry on Your work? And what will You do if this plan doesn't work? What's Your back-up plan?" Jesus said, **"I have no other plan -- it must work."** Truly, Jesus has no other plan than to depend on the efforts of His followers!

Today as we celebrate Jesus' Ascension into heaven, think about the GREAT COMMISSION. You and I are the ones who are Jesus' disciples in the world today. We're the ones who are supposed to spread His message with our lives and our words. We're the ones who are carrying on the work the Jesus began so many centuries ago. We're the ones who are now supposed to be fulfilling the GREAT COMMISSION. We believe in Jesus' teachings because those who came before us did their part. Now it's our turn.

I did that in a lot less than an hour-long sermon! I hope you don't feel cheated because it only took a few minutes! This is not new material. This is just a reminder of what all of us should be doing already. We are Jesus' disciples in the world today. It is up to us to continue His work. It's as simple as that! There is no back-up plan!

God bless you!

Pentecost

23 May 2010

FIRST READING: Acts 2:1-11
PSALM: Psalm 104:1, 24, 29-31, 34
SECOND READING: 1 Corinthians 12:3-7, 12-13
GOSPEL: John 20:19-23

God is even more likely to overdo things than I am!

What an exciting week in Paradise! And some really good food! I never knew that frying brussel sprouts in butter and olive oil could make them taste so good! But I ate a ton of them at one of our parishioner's homes. My 36th anniversary as a priest is coming up on Tuesday, and I hope that many of you will join me for the 8AM Mass at our church. Since I love to count things, that will be my 17994th Mass! I'm getting better at it! It's funny, but I remember a priest 36 years ago on my ordination retreat who told me and my class that he was PROUD that in all his years as a priest, he had NEVER eaten with ANY of his parishioners! I turned and told one of my classmates...."**If I can say that after a few months as a priest, just shoot me!**" I've been pretty good about eating with parishioners for the past 36 years. In fact, I got a donation request over the phone asking me to donate my old clothes to the hungry poor. My response was **"If they can fit in my clothes, they have not been hungry!"**

I was up in Vegas during the week and got to see 3 amazing shows......SPIKE AND HAMMER, OPEN SESAME, and THE LION KING. SPIKE AND HAMMER do a great family-friendly magic show at the Four Queens and I love their show! Lots of silly comedy and some great magic! OPEN SESAME is an amazing magic show at the Royal Resort. Four magicians doing their best stuff! I was in heaven (but Laughlin is still Paradise!). And THE LION KING was awesome, but the best part was going backstage after the show and meeting the actor who plays SCAR, the villain! Wickedly evil in the show, but a really nice guy off-stage. Turns out that he's Catholic, so he asked me to bless his dressing room! I've never blessed a dressing room before! There is actually a patron saint of actors....St. Genesius! He was a Roman actor who was converted on stage during a play because in the play he was doing the part of a Christian being martyred.....and he learned about Christianity and joined the Faith! Funny how things work out....

As you may already know, I have a tendency to overdo things. If I open a bag of peanuts intending to only eat only one, I know that very quickly I will be finished with most of the bag. If I see something on sale, I tend to not only buy one, but several just because they are such a good buy. Several of my friends called me when the new STAPLES commercial came out with the man going up to each item and saying **"WOW. WHAT A GREAT BUY!"** and then loading up his cart, and then doing the same thing with the next item. My friends asked if I had been the person who inspired STAPLES with the idea for that commercial since it was definitely me being depicted! In fact, they had a sale on pens, so I ended up buying 10 dozen of them. They were only $.50 a dozen! My only problem with this tendency to overdo things is that now I am running out of space!

And with the feast of Pentecost, the tendency to overdo things is also present. I'd love to fill the church with reminders of the Holy Spirit. I checked and there are three main symbols of the Holy Spirit in the Scriptures. He is depicted as a **DOVE** (hovering over Jesus during His baptism in the Jordan River), as a **FLAME OF FIRE** (enlightening the minds of the Apostles on Pentecost), and as a **WIND** (sending the breath of God's life into creation). Of course, filling the church with **DOVES, FLAMES and WIND** would not be a good idea! But one thought happily crossed my mind this week. See what you think of it. **God is even more likely to overdo things than I am!**

God gives to us so generously, generously beyond our belief. Look what He did for the Apostles on Pentecost in freeing them from fear and sending them out far and wide to all nations and peoples. Look at the different gifts and talents God has given to His people down through the ages. We all know people even today in our own parishes who face incredible hardships and difficulties with an amount of strength that can only come from God, not from themselves alone. **God gives to us so generously even when we only ask for a little. God will not be outdone in generosity to us.**

Today's Feast of Pentecost commemorates the fact that 50 days after Easter, Jesus sent the Holy Spirit upon the Apostles as a **GIFT** to strengthen them, to remove their fears, and to send them out on a mission. And while the Holy Spirit is the "Gift of the Father" to us, the Holy Spirit shares His presence and power with us in a variety of ways. The traditional **SEVEN GIFTS OF THE HOLY SPIRIT** remind us of some of those ways. I wonder how many of us actually remember them from our Catholic upbringing. Don't feel badly.....I had to look them up to be sure!

WISDOM - helps us to understand more deeply the truths of our Faith. God, because He is good, wants us to know about Him. He shares His truth with us through our Catholic Faith.

UNDERSTANDING - helps us to see all created persons and things in their relationship to God. Each human person is made in God's own image, even irrational creatures contain a "trace" of their Creator, human events lead us towards God.

COUNSEL - God even shares with us His Divine guidance so we can truly know which actions and thoughts are right, and which actions and thoughts are wrong.

FORTITUDE - strengthens our will-power so that with God's help we can stick to doing what is right and avoiding what is wrong even when it is difficult, or burdensome, or boring to do so.

KNOWLEDGE - gives us a greater understanding of God and His love for us.

PIETY - helps us to want to be in union with God and to worship Him faithfully. It is this gift which encourages us to pray, to attend Mass, to worship God.

FEAR OF THE LORD - produces in us a profound respect and reverence for God, and makes us want to avoid anything that would offend God. It is a healthy fear, a healthy respect, and it is for our benefit to respect and have reverence for God.

Like any other **GIFTS**, the **SEVEN GIFTS** of the Holy Spirit have to be received and have to be opened. We might wonder what is inside them, what they might do for us, but we actually have to open them and use them to really find out. We don't really know what this earth could be like if only we were to open up the **GIFTS** of the Holy Spirit and use them. All we do know is that God has promised us that with these gifts we can renew the face of the earth. Pray today that God's Holy Spirit may enlighten and strengthen each one of us, so we can appreciate the great gifts we have received, and that we will open them and use them in our lives.

A survey was done a few years ago about the types of prayers that Americans pray. It discovered that 85% of all prayers were prayers asking God for things. **GIVE ME THIS, GIVE ME THAT.** I was really upset about that survey because it seemed to indicate that the only time we ever go to God was when we wanted something from Him. But the more I have thought about it, the more it has seemed to me that there is another way of looking at that statistic. **IF WE GO TO GOD TO ASK HIM FOR SOMETHING FOR OURSELVES OR FOR OUR NEIGHBORS, AREN'T WE REALLY ADMITTING THAT WE NEED GOD?, that we can't do it without Him?** And doesn't today's feast of PENTECOST suggest that if we even open ourselves up to God's Spirit a little, God will give us so much more strength and help than we asked for.

God overdoes things far more than you and I do. God will not be outdone in generosity. Today let us celebrate Pentecost by really asking God for what we most need in our lives, and may we really feel God's tremendous generosity in answering our prayers beyond our wildest expectations.

I may need a lot more storage space to hold my bargains, but even the whole world cannot contain all that God offers to us through His Holy Spirit.

God bless you!

(On this weekend, I made the following announcement because of the bishop giving me an additional duty assignment at St. Francis of Assisi in Henderson.)

Please take home a copy of our parish bulletin and read the inserted page about my ADDITIONAL ASSIGNMENT. You get to read what I wrote, the people at St. Francis of Assisi in Henderson/Las Vegas have to sit through a 2 page letter from the bishop being read to them telling them about me! The bishop was very kind in what he wrote about me. In fact, I felt I should be laying dead in a casket hearing such good things! I will be meeting the parish staff there on Tuesday afternoon. The important thing for me, and hopefully for you, is that I am **NOT** leaving St. John the Baptist. I am being shared with St. Francis of Assisi. And I really think you are going to like Father John Assaloneassisting me at both parishes....he's only been a priest for one year, and, unlike me, he knows how to comb his hair! Please read the inserted page, and you will learn a little more of what is happening. We're excited about it! Now if we can just avoid being picked up by the highway patrol on Route 95 as we drive back and forth the 90 miles between the two parishes! But I guess staying within the speed limits is a good thing, so we'll be careful!

Double-Trouble!

Most Holy Trinity

30 May 2010

FIRST READING: Proverbs 8:22-31
PSALM: Psalm 8:4-9
SECOND READING: Romans 5:1-5
GOSPEL: John 16:12-15

So, here is more than you ever imagined you wanted to know about me!

(This sermon was the first sermon I preached at St. Francis of Assisi following my assignment there as Administrator.)

What an awesome weekend this is! Sure this is my first weekend at St. Francis of Assisi, but it is also the weekend on which I will celebrate my 18,000th Mass! I'm really proud of that! I never want to forget that offering each Mass is a tremendous gift and grace from God. There's a wonderful old saying that **"a priest should celebrate every Mass as if it were his First Mass and as if it were his last Mass."** I've always loved that thought. Over these past 36 years as a priest, I have been privileged to celebrate Mass in most of the 50 states (including Alaska and Hawaii), and in places as varied as Iceland, Turkey, Israel, Egypt, Italy, Germany, Holland, Austria, England, Macau, Hong Kong, Tahiti, Australia, New Zealand, Venezuela, the Virgin Islands, the Bahamas,

Bermuda, most of the larger Caribbean Islands, and even at St. Peter's Basilica in Rome. And whether Mass was offered in a little country church or in a huge basilica, each Mass reached up to God and brought God's love and power down to earth. **But in all this, I have never before celebrated Mass in Henderson!** So this is truly a first for me as well as a first for you! **And I want you to know from the very beginning of our relationship that I love being a priest!** I loved it on **May 25, 1974**, when I was ordained, and I love it even more today. And I am thrilled to be here with you as we embark on this adventure together. Father John and I will be taking care of St. John the Baptist in Laughlin as well as St. Francis of Assisi here in Henderson/Las Vegas. We will give you our best, and we ask for your prayers every day. And we promise our prayers for you. I've only met Father John a few times, but I am thankful to God for putting us together in this ministry. Life is an amazing and awesome adventure...and I'm thrilled that God has called all of us to share in this part of life's journey together. It's going to be an incredible ride!

I received a copy of the letter that was read to you at all the Masses last weekend. Bishop Pepe said such nice things about me. In fact, I never expected to hear such things said about me until I was dead and laying in my casket in church waiting for my funeral to begin! I will try to live up to the image that letter gave you of me, but like you I am only human!

I know you are curious....So let me tell you just a couple of things you might like to know about me. They are not religious things, they are just things.....I love **MAGIC**. No one loves magic more than I do! Living this close to Vegas is part of my dream come true! I was born and raised in New Jersey, but living in Nevada has always been my dream. And now that dream has come true!

I love to eat! I didn't get this shape without effort! A week or so ago, I received a phone call from some organization asking me to donate my old clothing to the hungry poor. I told the caller that if they could fit into my clothing, they weren't hungry! I should mention that I am not a big meat eater and never eat beef. It's not for health reasons....I'd just rather use my calories on things I really like....pasta, chocolate chip cookies, cheesecake...to name a few!

I am very proud to have served our great country in the United States Air Force as a chaplain, and I regard patriotism as a real virtue. The United States of America is not perfect, but it is my country, and I love this land. God bless the USA!

I love to talk, but I am learning to listen. I love jokes and I love to laugh. I worry that so many people take themselves much too seriously. God wants us to have joy in our lives. Golly, that was one of the hallmarks of St. Francis of Assisi so I know I am in the right place here!

I like to wear weird socks, wild colors and designs on them. Since I don't wear ties, socks are my only big color outlet! And I'm not sure what is happening with my hair! I used to have a crewcut, but now I'm experimenting with the wind-blown look! Eventually I will settle on something, just be patient!

And to leave you with a little sense of mystery about me, listen carefully to the following riddles about my life, and someday I will explain them: I am an only child, but I have a brother who is truly amazing. He lives in New York City and is about 20 years younger than I am. He sometimes has the wisdom of Solomon and I learn so much from him, but sometimes he just torments me! **His name is Michael**. I have never been married and I have never broken my vows, but I have a son right here in Nevada whom you will hear about in my sermons. He is in his 20's. **His name is Eddie.** Because of him, I know what parents go through! And I know why I have white hair! And I know what I put my parents through when I was a kid! Think about these mysteries....and someday I will explain Michael and Eddie to you.

I love to preach and I can remember 36 years ago when I preached my very first sermon. I asked a priest/friend of mine to comment on it afterwards, and this is what he said: **"I have three things to say to you about it.......It was read, it was read poorly, and it wasn't worth reading!"** I guess I should learn never to ask a friend's opinion!

Any priest enjoys hearing favorable comments about his sermons. Some time ago, a parishioner came up to me to talk after Mass. I thought that maybe I had said something which had particularly touched her heart, but she wasn't impressed with my theological clarity! She just wanted to tell me: **"You're so funny. Whenever I see you walking towards the pulpit, I start to laugh before you open your mouth! Thank you for brightening my week."** I guess there's some compliment in that! We preachers do reach people in different ways!

And God reaches us in a variety of ways too! Today's feast is called **TRINITY SUNDAY**, a day on which we celebrate the **MYSTERY OF THE HOLY TRINITY - THE MYSTERY OF THREE PERSONS IN ONE GOD.** It's a mystery because we don't fully understand it, but we do experience it, and every Sunday we say in the **CREED** that we believe in the **FATHER**, and the **SON**, and the **HOLY SPIRIT.** We experience God in our lives in many ways that reflect the **TRINITY.**

God is a loving and caring parent, a Father in the truest and most beautiful sense of the word. He created the world and He holds it in existence. He is all-powerful.

God is Jesus, a true human being, a person like us in all things but sin, a warm and personal friend to each one of us. He is close to us.

God is the Holy Spirit, an all-pervading presence, a power who enlightens our minds and strengthens our wills to do good and to avoid evil. He is God's gift of wisdom to each one of us.

Each one of us has his/her own way of relating to God or thinking about God. The **TRINITY** reminds us that we all need to relate to God in His **WHOLENESS**. He is a loving and caring Father, but He is also an **AWESOME JUDGE** who controls the entire universe. In Jesus, He is a truly human person like us, but He is **never** "just like us." He is always God among us. As the Holy Spirit, He is God's wisdom in the world, but He works through us and through others to share His wisdom and guidance. We need to pay attention to Him when he opens doors in our lives through people and events around us.

God is greater and larger than any of our categories for Him. He is beyond our categories of **TIME** and **SPACE**. He is the God who created the world, Who freed His people from slavery at the time of Moses, Who has in our own time chosen us as His own sons and daughters, and Who shares His own Spirit with us. **He will remain with us always.**

The simple sign of the cross which we make so often (and sometimes so very carelessly) is a powerful reminder that God always remains a mystery to us. He is Someone greater than we can ever imagine, Someone who cannot be confined to our narrow categories and our very limited minds.

God has made each one of us in His own image. We should never reverse things and try to make our God just like us. **God is higher, deeper, wider than even the universe itself....and for some reason in His eternal plan, God wants to be close to us!** Think of that the next time you make the sign of the cross. **God is higher, deeper, wider than even the universe itself....and for some reason in His eternal plan, God wants to be close to us!**

That is truly **AMAZING**! God wants to be close to you, and God wants to be close to me! If you take nothing else with you from Mass today, take that thought: **God is higher, deeper, wider than even the universe itself....and for some reason in His eternal plan, God wants to be close to us!**

And we should want to be close to Him!

God bless you!

In the Name of the Father, and of the Son, and of the Holy Spirit. Amen.

Corpus Christi

6 June 2010

FIRST READING: Genesis 14:18-20
PSALM: Psalm 110:1-4
SECOND READING: 1 Corinthians 11:23-26
GOSPEL: Luke 9: 11-17

You are what you eat! Yes, it's really true!

I'm really glad to be back here in Paradise for this weekend as we start to warm up for the summer. I think we're going to hit above 110 degrees today! Well, last weekend was my first weekend at St. Francis of Assisi in Henderson/Las Vegas. And it was their first chance to see me and hear me! If you want to see how I introduced myself to them, I printed the opening of my sermon in our bulletin this week. You've known me for a couple of years now, so you can see if I was telling them the truth or just selling myself to them! Let me know. Eddie showed up for one of the Masses with his beard and muscleshirt, and new dreadlocks, so I did get some questions about who that guy was who hugged me outside the church! I just told them that it's my son, and that kind of knocked them into a stunned silence!

I did all 6 of the weekend Masses there, and the least attended had over 500 people! The place is huge, but they seemed to like me. And I know

Father John had a great time here in Laughlin. We passed each other on Route 95 somewhere near Railroad Pass. I keep telling him it's only 90 miles between the two churches, and I've driven more than that just to go out for dinner! He's already billing himself as the younger version of me, so we're going to have some fun! He told one Mass here: **"I could be Father Charlie..just 40 pounds lighter and with dark hair."** I told the folks at St. Francis that **I was a preview of what Father John will look like in 15-20 years!** And I already got my first packet of food from the folks up there.....homemade Filipino noodles and rice. Let the feeding begin!

But I will have to come up with another nickname for Henderson/Las Vegas. **Laughlin is the only Paradise!** Don't worry, I'll think of something. Father John and I will be on retreat all this coming week up in Mesquite with all the priests from the Diocese of Las Vegas. Keep us all in your prayers. Last weekend, I celebrate two milestones....my 18,000th Mass, and my first anniversary of having a cellphone. After 18,000 Masses, I'm still awed by the power and the privilege of being a priest. And after a year with a cellphone, I have to admit that I don't know how I did without one for so long. I really hate to admit that! I'm becoming one of those people who write text messages with terrible spellings! Yet another reason to pray for me!

You know me, and I think it is a safe assumption on my part that there is probably no one else you know who enjoys talking about food more than I do. I love eating and I love eating out. (And no, that's not a hint for more Gift Certificates!) As you know, I never want recipes. **I don't want to know how to prepare the food; I just want to know people who know how to prepare the food!** I love pasta and cheese and ice cream and cake and fresh bread and chocolate chip cookies. Now I'm getting myself hungry! I like the feeling of being contentedly full!

There's no doubt about it, my friends, food and drink do affect us. There's even a wonderful old saying **"YOU ARE WHAT YOU EAT."** Of course, when I think of some of the food that I've consumed over the years...the peanut butter and banana pizzas, the cold egg rolls with hot mustard, the garlic ice cream, even the 3 day old reheated coffee, that particular saying can be frightening!

But down through the ages, God has come to mankind through food. Just think about it......**ADAM and EVE** were placed in a garden. **JOSEPH** stored the grain in Egypt to provide for his people in a time of famine. **MOSES** fed the Israelites with manna from heaven after they left Egypt. In today's Gospel, **JESUS** fed thousands of people with only a little bread and fish. And **JESUS** left us the Holy Eucharist, His own Body and Blood, in the form of bread and wine.

On this warm and beautiful weekend here in Paradise, I'd like to just suggest three simple reasons why I think God acted in this way throughout history, choosing to come to us down through the ages in signs connected with food. Here they are:

1. Because God knows our fascination with food. Almost all of our celebrations are somehow connected with food. Try to even imagine Christmas or Easter or Thanksgiving or a birthday or an anniversary without food! Even a funeral includes a repast after the burial. When we come together in joy or in sorrow, we like to eat.

2. Because God wants to remind us that we need Him daily, every day. None of us does without food for any great length of time. If supper is 10 minutes late, we complain that we're STARVING!

3. Maybe because God really believes that wonderful old saying I mentioned - **"YOU ARE WHAT YOU EAT!"** Think about that one this week. Maybe God wants us to become more like He is! That's why we don't eat or drink anything else for an hour before receiving Holy Communion. That's why we don't receive Holy Communion if we're living in a state of serious sin, that's why we make use of the sacrament of Confession to get ourselves out of that state of sin. Because in receiving Holy Communion, we are invited by God Himself to become like He is.

If you are fortunate enough to be able to receive Holy Communion today, just think about what God is inviting you to become - united with Him, united with God Who is the Source of all holiness. God couldn't possibly give us a greater gift than Himself. He literally puts Himself into our hands as well as into our bodies. God Himself joins Himself to us in a way that is possible only through receiving the **BODY AND BLOOD OF JESUS CHRIST** in the form of bread and wine.

This is why we gather together every Sunday, here in Paradise, up in Henderson/Las Vegas, or in any of the home parishes from which we come. This is why there is a priesthood. This really is why we are Catholic. The Holy Eucharist, the Body and Blood of Christ, is only available to us here. We have nothing more important to offer to you than the opportunity to be physically united with God Himself in Holy Communion. May we daily become more like God.**You are what you eat**. In receiving Holy Communion, we pray that this may really be true.

God bless you!

11th Sunday in Ordinary Time - "C"

13 June 2010

FIRST READING: 2 Samuel 12:7-10, 13
PSALM: Psalm 32:1-2, 5, 7, 11
SECOND READING: Galatians 2:16, 19-21
GOSPEL: Luke 7:36-8:3

"I like you.....I'll kill you last!"

Well, I'm sure it was an awesome week here in Paradise, but I was up in Mesquite with the priests of our diocese on a retreat for most of the week. Was amazed that on the Interstate 15 North of Las Vegas, the speed limit is actually 75 mph. Felt a little odd to be driving that fast and still be legal! And I wasn't even tempted to try to text message at that speed! Got to the hotel where we were all staying and I ended up with the one room that had a perfect view of the air-conditioning system! The hotel was not nearly full, so I asked if they could change it, but the hotel said no changes. So I had to content myself with good views of the mountains whenever I was outside my room. Unfortunately, the retreat speaker wasn't all that great. Many of us had some trouble staying awake, and it always bothers me that not only did I not understand the points the speaker was trying to make, but also that I don't think he understood them either. However, Father John and I amused ourselves by passing notes or text messages on our cellphones which we propped up and cleverly hid with our prayer books. We did an amazing quiz on the old I LOVE LUCY show. We almost got into trouble once when I sent a text message to the priest sitting in front of us that read: **"I like you....I'll kill you last!"** He looked at his phone, read the message, started to laugh out loud, and then turned around and glared at me and Father John! I guess the best compliment we got on the retreat was from one of the seminarians who sat near us who told us after one of the conferences, **"You two are crazy!"** But he ended up going out to dinner with us anyway.

The best part of the retreat was the time spent together with the other priests and seminarians of our Diocese of Las Vegas. The bishop stayed with us the whole retreat, and it ended up being a very good experience. Also found out there are 3 other priests in our diocese who are administering two parishes each, so I become the 4th one in our diocese to do this double duty. Thank goodness I have Father John with me, and with us, for this adventure.

In other events this week, several parishioners from St. John the Baptist drove up to Henderson/Las Vegas and visited St. Francis of Assisi. They were telling me how welcome they felt because of the staff and how beautiful the temporary church is. When I got back to St. Francis of Assisi, the staff were all telling me how friendly and happy the people were who visited from St. John the Baptist. Over the summer, Father John and I are hoping to plan some events for both parishes to experience together.

And while we were on retreat, the Chicago Blackhawks won the Stanley Cup for the first time since 1961! I had nothing to do with that, and actually had to ask what sport awards the Stanley Cup, but it sure made a lot of folks happy on the retreat and back in the parishes. I'll be waiting for the fall to see what the Steelers do. I know they play football. Someday I'll get that all straight in my mind.

Oh, last week, I mentioned that I needed to find another nickname for Henderson/Las Vegas, because Laughlin is the only real **PARADISE**. After one of the Masses, one of our parishioners suggested a solution. He said I should continue to call Laughlin **PARADISE**, and start calling Henderson/Las Vegas **PURGATORY**. Sorry, no-can-do, both are equally wonderful so the nicknames have to be more equal! But thanks for the suggestion!

A man was being tailgated on a busy street by an obviously stressed-out woman. When he didn't accelerate fast enough for her as a light turned green, she leaned on her horn and was screaming horrible things at him out her window. Red-faced, in mid-rant, she noticed a police officer tapping on her window. He ordered her out of her car, brought her to the police station where she was searched and fingerprinted, and placed in a holding cell. After a few hours, the arresting officer released her and said, "I'm terribly sorry for this mistake. You see, I pulled up behind your car while you were blowing your horn, gesturing rudely and cursing at the driver in front of you. I noticed the **"CHOOSE LIFE"** decal on your car, and the **"WHAT WOULD JESUS DO"** bumper sticker, and the **"THE FAMILY THAT PRAYS TOGETHER STAYS TOGETHER"** logo, so I naturally assumed you had stolen the car!

Actions speak louder than words. Our actions express our inner selves. This is what we find in today's gospel and other readings.

Invited to dine at a Pharisee's house, Jesus accepted. He knew it wasn't friendship that prompted the invitation, but the host wanted an opportunity to entrap Jesus and question Him about His religious teachings. But then, a notoriously sinful woman wanders into the dinner party, and pours her perfume on Jesus' feet and weeps, and acknowledges her sins. Unlike the Pharisee, this woman really welcomes Jesus into her heart. Her sins are forgiven and her life is changed.

Another biblical figure appears in the First Reading, a worse sinner than either the gospel woman or the tailgater. David, the King of Israel, is accused by the prophet Nathan of both adultery and murder. But David admits his sins (as bad as they were), and is forgiven.

So many sinful characters are put before us today: the rude tailgater (with the religious-looking stuff all over her car), the Pharisee who sets an elaborate feast to entrap Jesus, the forgiven woman who weeps over her sins at Jesus' feet, and King David who finally admits to being guilty of murder and adultery and is forgiven.

What's the lesson for us? Maybe you remember an old bumper sticker from the 1960's which read: **"IF IT WERE A CRIME TO BE A CHRISTIAN, WOULD THERE BE ENOUGH EVIDENCE TO CONVICT YOU?"** We have to ask ourselves some questions: **"Does my life really show the power of God's grace?"**.......**"Do my actions really show my belief in God?"**.......**"And though I sometimes stumble and fall, do I reach out for God's hand to lift me up, to forgive me, and to start over again?"**

We're all sinners because we're all human. We should all want to become saints. But the only real difference between a sinner and a saint is a really simple one. A saint is a sinner who keeps on trying. This is worth working on even as we enter the summer months. We can't take a vacation from trying to become the people God wants us to be.

Hang on to that thought: **A saint is a sinner who keeps on trying!**

God bless you!

12th Sunday in Ordinary Time - "C"

20 June 2010

FIRST READING: Zechariah 12:10-11, 13
PSALM: Psalm 63:2-6, 8-9
SECOND READING: Galatians 3:26-29
GOSPEL: Luke 9:18-24

Spending Father's Day at St. Francis of Assisi in Henderson was a beautiful experience. Here's what I preached there on this special day, using some of the SAME SERMON MATERIAL I had used at St. John the Baptist in Laughlin on the previous Sunday. I may not always be good at recycling things, but sometimes I do recycle words!

Well, it's a beautiful day here in the neighborhood. And it's a day on which we honor all fathers, grandfathers, great-grandfathers, God-fathers, stepfathers, and all those men who have in any way been like fathers to each one of us. You may be interested to learn that this year marks the 100th anniversary of the celebration of Father's Day! Sonora Dodd of Washington State first had the idea of a day for fathers. She wanted to honor her own father - William Dodd - a widowed Civil War Veteran - who after the death of his wife had raised their 6 children on his own. Since his birthday was in June, Sonora held the very first Father's Day celebration on June 19, 1910 in Spokane, Washington. It became a national celebration in 1966.

In honor of Father's Day, I've printed a list of some of my favorite quotations about fathers in today's bulletin. There are some humorous ones like this one from Bill Cosby - **"My father only hit me once - but he used a Volvo."** There are thoughtful ones like this one from Mark Twain - **"When I was a boy of four-teen, my father was so ignorant I could hardly stand to have the old man around. But when I got to be twenty-one, I was astonished at how much he had learned in seven years."** There are really insightful ones like this one from football coach Jim Valvano - **"My father gave me the greatest gift anyone could give another person, he believed in me."** And there is one awesome anonymous one that every father here should take into his own heart and mind - One night, a father overheard his son pray: **"Dear God, make me the kind of man my Daddy is."** Later that night, the father prayed: **"Dear God, make me the kind of man my son wants me to be."** So to all our fathers, grandfathers, great-grandfathers, Godfa-thers, step-fathers, and all those other men who have been like fathers to us....If they are still living, may God bless them in this life and if they have died, may God grant them joy in eternal life.

By the way, did you know that there are more COL-LECT phone calls on Father's Day than on any other day of the year?

Well, it's been two weeks since I was here for the Sunday Masses and during part of those two weeks, I was up in Mesquite with the priests of our diocese on a retreat for most of the week. Was amazed that on the Interstate 15 North of Las Vegas, the speed limit is actually 75 mph. Felt a little odd to be driving that fast and still be legal! And I wasn't even tempted to try to text message at that speed! Got to the hotel where we were all staying and I ended up with the one room that had a perfect view of the air-conditioning system! The hotel was not nearly full, so I asked if they could change it, but the hotel said no changes. So I had to content myself with good views of the mountains whenever I was outside my room. Unfortunately, the retreat speaker wasn't all that great. Some of us had some trouble staying awake, and it always bothers me that not only did I not understand the points the speaker was trying to make, but also that I don't think he understood them either. However, Father John and I amused ourselves by passing notes or text messages on our cellphones which we propped up and cleverly hid with our prayer books. We did an amazing quiz on the old I LOVE LUCY show. We almost got into trouble once when I sent a text message to the priest sitting in front of us that read: **"I like you....I'll kill you last!"** He looked at his phone, read the message, started to laugh out loud, and then turned around and glared at me and Father John! I guess the best compliment we got on the retreat was from one of the seminarians who sat near us who told us after one of the conferences, **"You two are crazy!"** But he ended up going out to dinner with us anyway.

The best part of the retreat was the time spent together with the other priests and seminarians of our Diocese of Las Vegas. Our bishop, Bishop Pepe, stayed with us the whole retreat, and it ended up being a very good experience because of that time together. Also found out there are 3 other priests in our diocese who are administering two parishes each, so I become the 4th one in our diocese to do this double duty. Thank goodness I have Father John with me, and with us, for this adventure.

In other events last week, several parishioners from St. John the Baptist drove up to Henderson/Las Vegas and visited St. Francis of Assisi. They were telling me how welcome they felt because of the staff and the people they met and how beautiful our temporary church is. When I got back to St. Francis of Assisi, the staff here were all telling me how friendly and happy the people were who visited from St. John the Baptist. Over the summer, Father John and I are hoping to plan some events for both parishes to experience together.

And while we were on retreat, the Chicago Blackhawks won the Stanley Cup for the first time since 1961! I had nothing to do with that, and actually had to ask what sport awards the Stanley Cup, but it sure made a lot of folks happy on the retreat and back in the parishes. I'll be waiting for the fall to see what the Steelers do. I know they play football.

A man was being tailgated on a busy street by an obviously stressed-out woman. When he didn't accelerate fast enough for her as a light turned green, she leaned on her horn and was screaming horrible things at him out her window. Red-faced, in mid-rant, she noticed a police officer tapping on her window. He ordered her out of her car, brought her to the police station where she was searched and fingerprinted, and placed in a holding cell. After a few hours, the arresting officer released her and said, "I'm terribly sorry for this mistake. You see, I pulled up behind your car while you were blowing your horn, gesturing rudely and cursing at the driver in front of you. I noticed the **"CHOOSE LIFE"** decal on your car, and the **"WHAT WOULD JESUS DO"** bumper sticker, and the **"THE FAMILY THAT PRAYS TOGETHER STAYS TOGETHER"** logo, so I naturally assumed you had stolen the car!

Actions speak louder than words. Our actions express our inner selves. This is a clear message in our readings today. In his letter to the Galatians, St. Paul writes: "You are all children of God in Christ Jesus....because you have clothed yourselves with Christ." What does it mean to be a Child of God? It means that we have to learn to think and act as Jesus would think and act. It means we have to put on Christ like we put on our clothing in the morning. It means that when people see us or hear us, they will see NOTHING that Christ Himself would not do, and hear NOTHING that Christ Himself would not say. It is our ACTIONS that show our FAITH. Otherwise, our faith is nothing but an empty show.

And in the Gospel, Jesus asks the disciples who they think He really is. And they answer correctly, but then Jesus goes on to tell them what this means, what they have to **DO** to be His disciples: **"If anyone wishes to come after Me, he must deny himself and take up his cross daily and follow me."** In other words, knowing **WHO** Jesus is is not what makes each of us a follower of Jesus. After all, even the **DEVIL** knows **WHO** Jesus is. But what makes each of us a follower of Jesus is our willingness to **DO** what He asks of us - deny ourselves, take up the crosses that come our way, and do our best to follow where Jesus is leading us.

What's the lesson for us? Maybe you remember an old bumper sticker from the 1960's which read: **"IF IT WERE A CRIME TO BE A CHRISTIAN, WOULD THERE BE ENOUGH EVIDENCE TO CONVICT YOU?"** We have to ask ourselves some questions: **"Does my life really show the power of God's grace?"**......."Do my actions really show my belief in God?"......."And though I sometimes stumble and fall, do I reach out for God's hand to lift me up, to forgive me, and to start over again?"**

After all, we're all sinners because we're all human. We should all want to become saints. But the only real difference between a sinner and a saint is a really simple one. A saint is a sinner who keeps on trying. This is worth working on even as we enter the summer months. We can't take a vacation from trying to become the people God wants us to be.

Hang on to that thought: **A saint is a sinner who keeps on trying!**

God bless you!

13th Sunday in Ordinary Time - "C"

27 June 2010

FIRST READING: 1 Kings 19:16, 19-21
PSALM: Psalm 16:1-2, 5, 7-8, 9-11
SECOND READING: Galatians 5:1, 13-18
GOSPEL: Luke 9:51-62

"It will be what you want it to be."

Another great week in Paradise! Besides enjoying some awesome vegetable lasagna and cheesecake and cinnamon rolls, I accomplished **two things** I have been working on. After almost two years of effort, I was finally able to crack the code on the parish website and begin updating it! And after several months, I was finally able to prod Eddie into getting his car registered with legitimate tags on it. Both are major accomplishments! The parish website was last updated in August 2007, so there was a lot of outdated information on it. I couldn't even get my name on it as Administrator! But I finally cracked the code and within a few weeks, we will have an updated and accurate website. It took me almost two years, but I didn't give up.

The last piece of the puzzle about the car registration was for Eddie to gather the documentation and take the documentation down to the court, pay the fine, and get on with his life. The night before he was scheduled to go, I had worked hard on encouraging him to gather all the paperwork, lay out the money he needed, and block out the time the next day to go and do it. After assuring me that he was gathering the paperwork, I went back to working on my computer. The next thing I know, I hear the TV blasting downstairs. I came down like a banshee! Now I really know how parents feel.....I was yelling what my Mom used to yell: **"There will be no TV, young man, until you find those papers and get all the stuff laid out for tomorrow!"** Well, he finally did it. And I felt so good! It took months, but I didn't give up!

Late one night this past week, I was having dinner at the Peppermill in Las Vegas at about 2:00AM with some good friends. We got to discussing what our parents did to punish us if we did something wrong as kids. One guy spoke about his parents spanking him, another talked about being sent to his room. When they asked me, I at first tried to explain that I had never done anything wrong as a kid, but they didn't buy that! So I explained that my Mom would throw the parrot at me. One guy choked on his dinner while the others asked me to explain. When I didn't do something my Mom had asked, she would calmly get a big yardstick, go to the parrot's cage, and the parrot would climb onto the yardstick. She would then hurl the parrot at me who would land on me with his claws outstretched. This was particularly effective if I didn't want to get out of bed on time. There I would be bouncing around in bed trying to unattach the parrot's claws from me. I can still remember my Mom saying: **"Don't make me get the parrot!"** Hmmm....maybe I need to buy a parrot for when I'm talking to Eddie.....

In our First Reading today, Elijah calls Elisha to follow him and not let anything get in the way of his following. In our Second Reading today, St. Paul reminds us that we need to stand firm as we follow Christ, and not give in to any other desires. And in the Gospel, Jesus reminds us not to look back, but to keep moving forward in our journey to become the people God wants us to be. There will always be obstacles to loving our neighbors because sometimes our neighbors are not all that lovable. There will always be obstacles to growing into the people God wants us to be because there are always other things competing for our attention. So we have to keep our focus. We have to know and resolve to commit ourselves to the constant effort that living as a Catholic Christian involves. It won't always be easy, but it will always be worthwhile.

Thinking about the readings and the parrot reminded me of a story I told years ago at a graduation. I think it still makes a good point for us to think about today.

In a small village, there was an old man who had a reputation for being very wise. Two young boys decided they wanted to have some fun and embarrass the old man. So they came up with a plan. They would catch a young bird and one of the boys would place it between his cupped hands. They would go up to the old man and ask him in front of the villagers, **"Is the bird dead or alive?"** If the old man said that the bird was dead, the boy would open his hands and show the live bird. If the old man said that the bird was alive, the boy would crush his hands together before opening them, and show the dead bird. When they came to the old man in front of he villagers, they asked him the question: **"Is the bird dead or alive?"** and he looked into their eyes, knew what was in their hearts, and simply responded: **"It will be what you want it to be."**

That's pretty much the lesson for us about our dedication to following Jesus and not letting anything get in the way of loving our neighbors and loving God. **It will be what you want it to be.**

God bless you!

14th Sunday in Ordinary Time - "C"

4 July 2010

FIRST READING: Isaiah 66:10-14
PSALM: Psalm 66:1-3,4-5,6-7, 16, 20
SECOND READING: Galatians 6:14-18
GOSPEL: Luke 10:1-12, 17-20

Back at St. Francis of Assisi for the 4th of July Weekend! And once again, I have recycled some words from what I had said at St. John the Baptist in Laughlin on another Sunday.

We received word on Friday that Bishop Pepe has assigned Father Steve Hoffer as a parochial vicar here at St. Francis. In this day and age, having TWO parochial vicars is almost unheard of! Having two parochial vicars as young as Father John and Father Steve is infinitely more rare! But our status as a growing parish surely justifies it. So we are very grateful that as of August 1st, St. Francis of Assisi will have two young parochial vicars.....and one aging administrator!

On this July 4th weekend, I know I don't need to give a long sermon and you don't need to sit for one either. But I'd like to point out a bit of inspiration as we celebrate our 234th birthday as a free and independent nation. The Declaration of

Independence, which was signed 234 years ago, begins with this stirring words:

"We hold these truths to be self-evident, that all men are created equal, that they are endowed by their Creator with certain unalienable Rights, that among these are Life, Liberty and the pursuit of Happiness."

234 years later, we all need to remember from the very beginning, our nation has acknowledged there is a **CREATOR**, and He is the Source of all our rights. And that we are all endowed by our Creator with the right to **LIFE**, **LIBERTY** and the **PURSUIT OF HAPPINESS**. The Declaration of Independence states that all of this is **SELF-EVIDENT**, meaning any thinking person should be able to see it.

So as we celebrate this July 4th weekend, it's good for us to give thanks to our **CREATOR,** and to thank Him for giving us **LIFE**, and **LIBERTY**, and allowing us to pursue our happiness. It should be **SELF-EVIDENT** to all of us that God has given us to very much in the course of our lives. It's good to think about this.

There are websites for everything these days. There's one for waiters called **WAITER'S REVENGE** where waiters and waitresses can post the most annoying things that customers in restaurants have done to them.....and what funny or disgusting things they have done to get even! It's worth checking out, but it may make you a little worried about eating out for awhile!

There are many sites for preachers, and one listed some comments about sermons. I really enjoyed that one, even though it made me think a bit about my own preaching style.

The definition of a good sermon: It should have a good beginning. It should have a good ending. And they should be as close together as possible.

A sermon should be modeled on a woman's dress: long enough to cover the subject, but short enough to be interesting.

A rule of thumb for preachers: If after ten minutes you haven't struck oil, stop boring!

A woman said, "Father, that was a very good sermon!" The priest says, "Oh, I have to give the credit to the Holy Spirit." And the woman replied, "It wasn't THAT good!"

A priest, whose sermons were very long and boring, announced in the church one Sunday that he had been transferred to another church, and it was Jesus' wish that he leave that week. The congregation got up and sang, "What a Friend We Have in Jesus!"

So, with that in mind, on to today's sermon.....

There once was a king who offered a prize to the artist who would paint the best picture of **PEACE**. Many artists tried. The king looked at all the pictures. But there were only two he really liked, and he had to choose between them. One picture was of a calm lake. The lake was a perfect mirror for peaceful towering mountains all around it. Overhead was a blue sky with fluffy white clouds. All who saw this picture thought that it was a perfect picture of peace. The other picture too had mountains, but they were rugged and bare. Above was an angry sky, from which rain fell and in which lightning played. Down the side of the mountain tumbled a foaming waterfall. This did not look peaceful at all! But when the king looked closely, he saw behind the waterfall a tiny bush growing in a crack in the rock. In the bush a mother bird had build her nest. There, in the midst of the rush of angry water, sat the mother bird on her nest...in perfect peace.

Which picture do you think won the king's prize? The king chose the second picture. Do you know why? **"Because,"** explained the king, **"peace does not mean to be in a place where there is no noise, trouble or hard work. Peace means to be in the midst of all those things and still be calm in your heart. This is the real meaning of peace."**

Today's Gospel reading from St. Luke tells us that the 72 disciples were sent out two-by-two to bring

His message of peace. They were to strengthen and support each other, to depend on God for what they needed, and to share God's message with those to whom they were sent. They were even reminded that they would not always be successful, but they should never give up, or become cynical. They had a message that was incredibly valuable. And they were never to stop offering it to the world.

The lessons for us are simple and obvious. Think of that picture of peace, realize that your Faith gives you the ability to face whatever life throws at you, learn to depend on God more than Anyone else and never give up on sharing your Faith with those around you in whatever ways you can.

Like Jesus' original disciples, we too have a message for the world that is incredibly valuable. And we are never to stop offering it to the world. It is a message that is more powerful, more life-changing, more hopeful than even our Declaration of Independence! It can bring us to eternal life, complete liberty from sin, and everlasting happiness.

God bless you!

Made in the USA
Middletown, DE
14 July 2021

44036146R10190